W. H. TUCKER &

Yellow Funnel Fleet

1920   PLEASURE   SAILINGS   1920

(Weather and other circumstances permitting).

From ILFRACOMBE & LYNMOUTH by the Magnificent Saloon Steamers

'LADY MOYRA,' 'LADY EVELYN' & 'ROBINA'

(The Largest and Fastest).

Whit-Monday, May 24th.	**Single Trip to Lynmouth, Minehead, and Cardiff.** Leaving ILFRACOMBE 6-15 p.m. Off Lynmouth 6-45 p.m. Steamer leaves Cardiff 9-30 a.m. Minehead 10-15 a.m. Off Lynmouth 11-15 a.m. **Grand Cheap Afternoon Cruise.** Allowing about 2½ hours on the water. Leaving ILFRACOMBE 2-30 p.m. FARE 2/-
Whit-Tuesday, May 25th	**Single Trip to Lynmouth, Minehead, and Cardiff.** Leaving ILFRACOMBE 7-30 p.m. Off Lynmouth 8-0 p.m. Steamer leaves Cardiff 10-0 a.m. Minehead 11-15 a.m. Off Lynmouth 1-45 a.m. **Special Cheap Afternoon Cruise.** Allowing about 2½ hours on the water. Leaving ILFRACOMBE 2-30 p.m. FARE 2/-
Wednesday May 26th.	**Single Trip to Lynmouth, Minehead, and Cardiff.** Leaving ILFRACOMBE 7-40 p.m. Off Lynmouth 4-15 p.m. Minehead 9-10 p.m. Steamer leaves Cardiff 9-50 a.m. Minehead 11-15 a.m. Off Lynmouth 11-45 a.m. **Afternoon Trip to Lynmouth.** Allowing 3 hours ashore. Leave ILFRACOMBE 2-30 p.m. Steamer leaves Lynmouth 6-15 p.m. FARE 4/6
Saturday, May 29th.	**Single Trip to Lynmouth, Weston, and Cardiff.** Leaving ILFRACOMBE 3-45 p.m. Off Lynmouth 4-15 p.m. Steamer leaves Cardiff 8-00 a.m. Off Lynmouth 11-15 a.m.
Monday, May 31st.	**Single Trip to Lynmouth & Cardiff.** Leaving ILFRACOMBE 4-0 p.m. Off Lynmouth 4-30 p.m. Steamer leaves Cardiff 9-35 a.m. Off Lynmouth 11-10 a.m.

FARES :   ILFRACOMBE to LYNMOUTH, or vice versa, Single **4/6**   ILFRACOMBE to WESTON (Single), **6/-**
ILFRACOMBE or LYNMOUTH to CARDIFF, Single **6/-**, Tourist **10/-**
LYNMOUTH to ILFRACOMBE, Day Return **4/6**.

NOTE.—Fares from Lynmouth do not include landing or embarking at Lynmouth.

Bicycles, Prams, Mail Carts (at owner's risk) **2/-** each way. Motor Cycles (Petrol Tank must be empty) **4/-** each way (Side Cars which must be detached) **2/-** each way.

Children under 12 Half-Price for all Trips.

SPECIAL EXCURSIONS

FRONT COVER:- The WESTWARD HO ploughs through heavy seas as she steams down the Bristol Channel. (Detail from an original oil painting by Chris Collard).

BACK COVER:- The DEVONIA at anchor off Newquay, (Cornwall). (Detail from an original oil painting by Chris Collard).

The BRITANNIA at Bridge Wharf, Glasgow. October 1920. (TBT)

SPECIAL EXCURSIONS
WHITE FUNNELS – VOLUME TWO
The story of Campbells' Steamers 1919 - 1939
BY
CHRIS COLLARD

Captain Alec Campbell (CCC)

Captain Peter Campbell (CCC)

WHEELHOUSE BOOKS.
4, Ty Mawr Close,
Rumney,
Cardiff.
CF3 8BU.

PUBLISHED BY WHEELHOUSE BOOKS
PRODUCED BY WILPRINT GROUP LTD.
BOOKBINDING BY CEDRIC CHIVERS LTD.
COVER DESIGN BY PETER H. JONES, WILPRINT GROUP LTD.

ISBN 0-9534275-0-1

CONTENTS

ACKNOWLEDGEMENTS

The major part of the contents of this second volume of White Funnel Fleet history has been taken from the extensive records of P. & A. Campbell Ltd., now held in the Bristol Records Office. I wish to express my thanks to the Bristol City Archivist, Mr. John Williams, and his staff for their willing assistance.

The scrapbooks of Mr. Sydney Robinson have once again been made available to me and have been a source of invaluable information. Similarly, the diaries of Miss Gwyneth White, of Penarth, have been placed at my disposal and I am most grateful for her permission to quote freely from them. I also wish to acknowledge the help of Mr. Richard Clammer, particularly with regard to the company's South Devon sailings, and Mr. Nigel Coombes for contributing the foreword, written in his characteristically eloquent style.

Dr. Donald Anderson, Chairman of the Bristol Channel branch of the Paddle Steamer Preservation Society, has given me every encouragement and I am especially grateful for his permission to use information concerning the Yellow Funnel Fleet and the Lady Rowena, which first appeared in his articles in "Ship Ahoy", the former magazine of the South Wales branch of the World Ship Society.

My good friend Mr. George Owen, the doyen of Bristol Channel historians, has again been of invaluable assistance and has contributed much to this volume, not only in checking the manuscript with his own meticulous records but also by way of his wealth of personal reminiscences. My debt of gratitude to him is enormous.

Key to Caption Credits

HAA	H. A. Allen	BMC	Bryn May Collection
TBT	The Ballast Trust	HGO	George Owen
ERK	Edwin Keen	FP	Fred Plant
GEL	Graham Langmuir	SR	Sydney Robinson

It has been impossible to establish the source of a number of the photographs: these are denoted - CCC - Chris Collard Collection. I hope that this "omnibus" acknowledgement will be accepted by the individual photographers concerned in appreciation of their work and their valuable contributions to this history.

DEDICATION

This work is dedicated to my mentor, Mr. George Owen, with sincere gratitude for over thirty years of continuing friendship.

FOREWORD

A complete history of the White Funnel steamers has been long overdue. Chris Collard's review of the years 1946 - 1968, in his first book, was an outstanding success.

The story of White Funnels in the inter-war years of 1919 - 1939, this excellent volume, presents more of a challenge to the historian.

The events have to be painstakingly recreated from sources beyond contemporary spoken memories, though happily there are still some wonderfully sharp recollections to call upon.

Then there is the excitement of putting it all together and digging out those priceless rare photographs to illustrate it. That excitement and thoroughness are qualities which Chris Collard has again brought to the fore in what has, for him, been a lifelong enthusiasm.

His readers will thank him for rescuing information that in the ensuing years might well have disappeared without trace: that is the importance of people like Chris. To be a guardian of the past is to help safeguard the future.

A mere fifteen years ago it is doubtful whether a book of this kind would have excited a publisher. In the dying days of the Campbell flag the Bristol Channel pleasure steamer tradition had sunk to a whisper. The arrival of PS Waverley and, later, MV Balmoral changed all that. The exhilaration of today's trips down the Channel has re-awakened a healthy interest in what it used to be like, the more assured present feeding on the delights of the past. It really is a wonderful story.

Future volumes in the series will open up the shadowy movements of Campbells' steamers in the two World Wars, periods only perfunctorily explored. But, for now, enjoy the peaceful years, the inter-war years, which consolidated P & A Campbell Ltd. as the greatest excursion fleet in British waters.

Nigel Coombes.
Vice-President, Paddle Steamer Preservation Society.

INTRODUCTION

On a warm and sunny morning at a seaside resort somewhere in Great Britain, holidaymakers converge on the pier. Their attention is drawn to a paddle steamer rounding the point a few miles away. As she approaches the pier her paddles stop and she glides smoothly alongside the landing stage. Ropes are thrown ashore, the gangways are quickly run out and the passengers stream aboard. The white funnels, the brass and the varnished wood gleam in the sunlight; the promenade deck is still wet after scrubbing and washing down by the crew. There is the gentle hiss of her full head of steam, and the smell of breakfast, being served in the dining saloon, mingles with the salty tang of the sea air. The master leans over the wing of the bridge, watching the last of the passengers embark. The gangways are taken aboard and the telegraph rings; the ropes are cast off and the ship is on her way. The bystanders on the pier watch her sail into the distance with the white wake bubbling and frothing behind her.

Such scenes were enacted on countless occasions at countless locations during the years between the wars; that Great British Institution - the seaside holiday - was in full swing! However, the happy and carefree exterior concealed a troubled and uncertain time.

The Great War brought about widespread changes which had an irrevocable effect on society. Initially it appeared that little had changed, but the optimism at the end of the conflict faded as economic breakdown and political uncertainty took hold. More and more workers rebelled at the old order of the pre-war days and industrial unrest became rife.

With the 1930's came the depression; unemployment soared in most European countries and with it came the evils of poverty and unrest. The politics of depression became the politics of war and over the whole decade there hung, like a darkening cloud, the spectre of impending hostility.

Against this daunting background the steamers of the White Funnel Fleet continued to operate their services in the Bristol Channel and on the South Coast. The financial constraints of the period were compounded by much bad weather, however, efficient management and a carefully planned network of sailings more than satisfied the demands of the public. The ships, maintained to the highest standards, and the expertise of their personnel ensured that the company continued to uphold the reputation for which it had become so justly renowned.

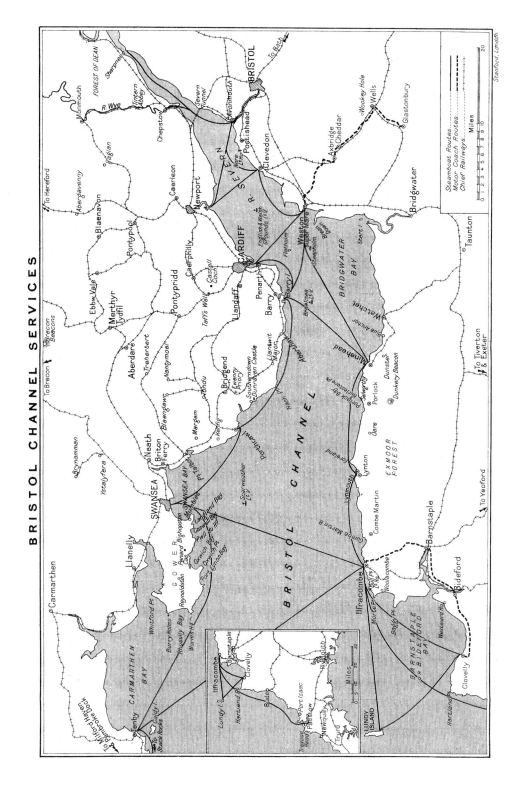

The Bristol Channel routes from The White Funnel Handbook. 1939.

9

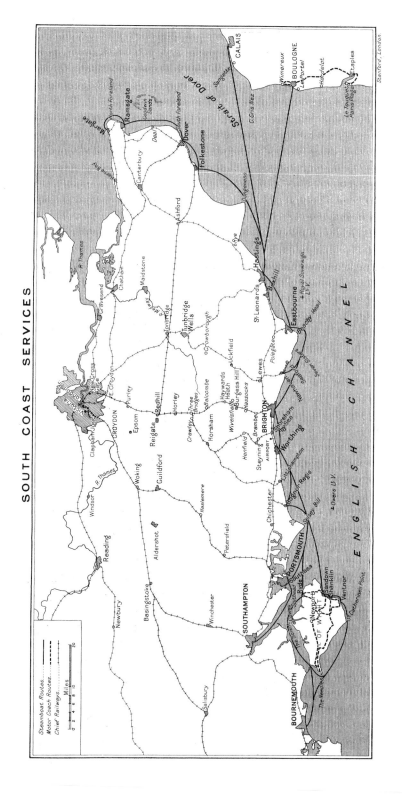

The South Coast routes from The White Funnel Handbook. 1939.

Chapter 1 – 1919/1920

The Golden Age of the British paddle steamer ended during the summer of 1914 with the outbreak of the First World War. The White Funnel Fleet then consisted of thirteen vessels, all of which were eventually taken over by the Admiralty for minesweeping and other duties.

During the summers of 1917 and 1918 a solitary, white-funnelled vessel plied the waters of the Bristol Channel. She was the **DUCHESS OF DEVONSHIRE,** the small paddle steamer chartered from the Devon Dock, Pier and Steamship Co. Ltd. to maintain P. & A. Campbell's Cardiff to Weston ferry.

The Great War ended with the Armistice of November 11th. 1918, but the surviving vessels of the White Funnel Fleet were retained for use on the post-war Mine Clearance Scheme. Sadly, the **BRIGHTON QUEEN** and the **LADY ISMAY** had been lost while on active service but the others, having completed their naval operations, eventually returned to their home port of Bristol and prepared for their return to civilian service.

The pattern which the 1919 season would adopt depended on the availability of the steamers following their refits. In view of the consequent uncertainty the company decided to continue the charter of the **DUCHESS OF DEVONSHIRE.** Under the command of Capt. J. J. Ashford, she opened the season on Wednesday 4th. June, just before Whitsun, but her sole operation on the Cardiff to Weston ferry was brief.

Saturday 14th. June 1919 was an eventful day; the national newspapers reported that Alcock and Brown had taken off on what was to become the first non-stop flight across the Atlantic. The other "first" of that day, while hardly an event of national importance, was to have significant repercussions on Bristol Channel history - it was the day the opposition arrived, in the form of Tucker's Yellow Funnel Fleet!

In the 1880's William Henry Tucker entered the shipping scene in Cardiff as a tug owner, with interests in salvage and sand dredging, as well as running a shore business as an anchor and chain merchant. He died in December 1914, but his three sons, Arthur Reginald, Gerald Maxwell and Ernest Vivian, inherited the business.

In 1919 Reg Tucker saw the possibilities of entering the excursion trade from Cardiff and the company purchased two widely contrasting paddle steamers from the Furness Railway. They were the **LADY EVELYN** and the **LADY MOYRA;** both of them, incidentally, named after the wives of two of that company's directors.

The **LADY EVELYN** had been built and engined by John Scott & Co. of Kinghorn in 1900, originally of 170ft. in length and a gross tonnage of 295. She was, however, rebuilt in 1904 by Vickers Sons and Maxim Ltd., at Barrow-in-Furness. Her open foredeck was plated in and she was lengthened to 200ft., which increased her gross tonnage to 320. In the Bristol Channel she was to be employed mostly on the Cardiff to Weston ferry where she was certificated to carry a maximum of 749 passengers.

The **LADY MOYRA** was none other than the former **GWALIA,** built in 1905 by John Brown of Clydebank, for the Barry Railway Co., and arch-rival of the P. & A. Campbell steamers. She had been sold to the Furness Railway in 1910, and like the **LADY EVELYN,** operated on the Barrow to Fleetwood service. With her length of 245ft. and gross tonnage of 519 she was certificated to carry up to 1133 passengers in the upper reaches of the Bristol Channel. Her double-ended boiler with its eight furnaces, closed stokehold and forced draught led to high coal consumption of about 2½ tons per hour at full speed. Her operating costs were high, compared with the very economical **LADY EVELYN** but she was much faster, and her turn of speed enabled her to compete on even terms with the "flyers" of the White Funnel Fleet.

The **LADY EVELYN** arrived at Cardiff on Monday 9th. June 1919 and, under the command of Capt. Bob Case, inaugurated the Yellow Funnel Fleet's services on Saturday 14th. June.

On her first day she embarked a total of 692 passengers for Weston while the **DUCHESS OF DEVONSHIRE** embarked 842, but for the next week, when the two ships had the channel to themselves, the Yellow Funnel steamer carried the cream of the trade. No doubt the public were eager to try the facilities of the new company.

And good those facilities were! The catering on both steamers was excellent, as was the custom on all Bristol Channel ships of the period. On entering the dining saloon the passengers were faced with tables laden with cold joints and a whole Severn salmon. First class cooked luncheons were provided at 2/6d or 3/- and teas were served for 2/6d or 2/-. The 2/- tea consisted of as much cold meat and salad, with bread and butter and jam and as many cups of tea or coffee as one wished. For the 2/6 tea, salmon was served before the meat. Plaice and chips were always available as an alternative and second helpings were always offered. There was little or no profit on such lavish catering but the food was a great attraction and good money was to be made in the bars.

The first of the White Funnel steamers to be refitted was the **RAVENSWOOD**, which entered service from Cardiff on the afternoon of Saturday 21st. June. Almost immediately, racing ensued between the rival vessels and the company's memorandum books, which record the day to day activities of each steamer, contain many notes such as the following:

> "Lady Evelyn left Weston one length ahead of Ravenswood at 14.00. Ravenswood passed her and was three lengths ahead passing Penarth."

The Ailsa Shipbuilding Co. Ltd. completed the refit of the **GLEN AVON** by early July. She left Troon for Bristol on Saturday 5th. July, under the command of Capt. Daniel Ryan, and arrived at Bristol on Monday 7th. The **LADY MOYRA** arrived in Cardiff from Barrow-in-Furness on Thursday 10th. July and over the next couple of days the following advertisements appeared in the Cardiff newspapers:-

Western Mail. Thursday 10th. July 1919.

"TRIPS TO ILFRACOMBE

Messrs. W. H. Tucker are resuming the Channel service from Cardiff to Ilfracombe next week. A new steamer - the Lady Moyra - will then be in commission.

There is only one stipulation imposed by the authorities in regard to these trips and that is that they must be run in daylight and the navigators must be able to see two miles ahead. This precaution is doubtless on account of mines but it does not mean that there are mines in the channel. The order is not imposed for the Bristol Channel alone but is a general one and any nervousness on this ground is unnecessary.

Messrs. Campbells Glen Avon has undergone her refit and trials at Troon and reached Bristol on Monday last. She will be in commission very shortly."

Western Mail. Saturday 12th. July 1919.

"CHANNEL BOAT TRIPS

Messrs. P. & A. Campbell are able to resume their pre-war sailings of pleasure boats to the Bristol Channel resorts. Up to the present Weston has been the sole port of call. But from Monday onwards, Ilfracombe with Minehead and Lynmouth en route, and Clovelly with Bristol and Clevedon will again be placed on the programme of the White Funnel Fleet. The Glen Avon makes her first trip today, to Weston, and next week proceeds down channel...".

The **LADY MOYRA** entered service on Saturday 12th. July. On her initial sailing she took 363 passengers to Weston and arrived back in Cardiff in time to make a run, at 10.30, to Ilfracombe with 58 passengers. She arrived at 13.05 and, to celebrate the occasion, made a complimentary cruise out of Ilfracombe with nearly 300 passengers. She was commanded by Capt. J. W. (Jimmy) James, a well known Bristol Channel master who had been her first captain in her Barry Railway days from 1905.

The **GLEN AVON** also entered service on Saturday 12th. July and on that day, while Tucker's landed 1049 passengers at Weston, the larger Campbell fleet landed 3396.

At first, fares by both companies to Weston were 3/6d single and 5/day return, but commencing on Friday 11th. July, Tucker's were advertising cheap evening trips to Weston at 2/-, and Campbell's quickly followed suit. Both companies introduced 5/-period returns, Tucker's on a weekly basis and Campbell's on a weekend basis.

The rivalry between the two companies became intense and racing became a daily occurrence, although strenuously denied by all concerned. On the day the **GLEN AVON** entered service, although leaving Cardiff 4 minutes after the **LADY EVELYN,** she passed her just over half way to Weston. On St. Swithin's Day, Tuesday 15th. July, the **RAVENSWOOD** left Cardiff 3 minutes behind the **LADY EVELYN** but was half a length ahead off Weston. One can only imagine the language aboard the White Funnel steamer when the Pier Master allowed the **LADY EVELYN** into the pier first! On those races, Chief Engineer Bill Brown, of the **LADY EVELYN,** would promise his firemen a flagon of beer if they won the pier and sometimes they received it, even if they lost, for their valiant efforts.

The real racing, however, took place on the Ilfracombe route. The **LADY MOYRA** left Cardiff at 09.35 whenever possible, nine or ten days out of the fourteen days of the tidal cycle, for Minehead, Lynmouth, Ilfracombe and Clovelly. The first encounter resulted in a resounding victory for the **LADY MOYRA** when, on Wednesday 16th. July, she ran down channel with the **GLEN AVON.** The latter reached Minehead first and the **LADY MOYRA** was ten minutes behind her when she left the pier, but she overhauled the White Funnel ship and was two minutes ahead arriving at Ilfracombe Pier.

However, retribution was at hand! The next steamer to enter service was the **CAMBRIA.** Under the command of Campbell's senior master, Capt. Daniel Taylor, she began by taking the first sailing from Bristol to Ilfracombe on Saturday 2nd. August 1919.

The **LADY MOYRA** had beaten the **GLEN AVON** in several races down channel but was now more evenly matched by the **CAMBRIA;** two old adversaries from the pre-war days reunited, setting the scene for some dramatic encounters.

On Monday 11th. August the **LADY MOYRA** was scheduled to sail to Ilfracombe via Minehead but this intermediate call was omitted when it was learned that the **CAMBRIA** was going direct. (Little regard appears to have been paid to the passengers waiting on Minehead Pier!). This was the **CAMBRIA'S** day; she left Cardiff at 09.41 followed by the **LADY MOYRA** 4 minutes later. The **CAMBRIA** was off the Foreland at 11.13 but the **LADY MOYRA** was twenty minutes behind. Although the **CAMBRIA** called at Lynmouth and the **LADY MOYRA** apparently did not, the White Funnel steamer arrived at Ilfracombe at 12.19, some 17 minutes ahead.

On Thursday 14th. August the **LADY MOYRA** left Cardiff at 09.32 and the **CAMBRIA** at 09.38. The White Funnel steamer passed the **LADY MOYRA** at 10.25 and arrived at Minehead first, picking up all the passengers. In doing so she explained the whole purpose of racing - more then mere prestige was involved!

The **GLEN USK**, following her refit, left Glasgow under the command of Capt. J. H. Denman, for compass adjusting, on Wednesday 3rd. September. She called at Kilmun that afternoon before sailing for Bristol in readiness to make her first trip, to Cardiff, Lynmouth and Ilfracombe, on Saturday 6th. September.

The **LADY MOYRA** paid her first visit to Mumbles on Wednesday 10th. September, from Cardiff, via Ilfracombe. The trip was run specially to view the Battleship **QUEEN ELIZABETH,** and the Battle Cruisers, **TIGER** and **LION,** at anchor in Swansea Bay on a courtesy visit. It had been planned for passengers to board the **QUEEN ELIZABETH** but the warship had lost an anchor and the boarding was cancelled. On the following day, however, the **LADY MOYRA** ran a similar trip, incorporating two cruises from Mumbles, to board the **LION,** on which she carried a total of 1600 passengers.

The end of the Yellow Funnel Fleet's first summer season was marred by a series of unfortunate events. In the early part of August they introduced extra sailings, at short notice, to which the Cardiff Dock Master took exception and they were consequently forced to revert to their original schedules at the end of the month. This caused much confusion with the travelling public and Campbell's drew special attention, in the newspapers, to the fact that their sailings were unchanged.

On the evening of Saturday 20th. September, while approaching Weston pier, the **LADY EVELYN'S** steering gear jammed. She was immediately stopped and began to drift in the direction of Steep Holm. The **LADY MOYRA,** on her way up from Ilfracombe, went alongside and took off all her passengers. The **LADY EVELYN** remained at anchor while temporary repairs were effected and she eventually reached Cardiff under her own steam.

Two days later the **LADY MOYRA** fouled a buoy outside the Queen Alexandra Dock, Cardiff, bending two floats and three radius rods in the starboard paddle wheel. She was off service on the 23rd. and 24th. September, and although she made a test run to Weston on the morning of Thursday 25th. she was cancelled for the rest of the day.

On the following evening the **LADY EVELYN** was involved in a collision, but despite investigation no further information has been ascertained regarding the details of this incident. She was taken out of service, however, and did not resume sailing that year.

Throughout 1919 industrial unrest began to grow and culminated in a national rail strike, which commenced on Saturday 27th. September, and which eventually forced 600,000 people out of work. The coal supply situation brought about a serious reduction of services by both fleets. The **LADY MOYRA** ended her season on Thursday 2nd. October but Campbell's, who held a bigger coal reserve, were able to carry on and survive the nine days of the strike.

The **DUCHESS OF DEVONSHIRE,** after sailing out of Newport since the beginning of September, completed her charter at the end of that month and left Bristol on the morning of Thursday 2nd. October to return to her owners. After being forced to shelter in Barry Roads until 06.00 on Friday 3rd. October, she passed Ilfracombe at 10.00, rounded Land's End at 19.30 and arrived at Exmouth at 10.00 on the following day.

The season, which had been one of very fine weather, was closed by the **GLEN AVON** on Saturday 11th. October, but there then followed a unique chapter of its own.

Tucker's had enjoyed a very profitable summer and it was decided to increase the fleet for the following year. The twin screw steamer **ROBINA** of 306 gross tons, built by the Ardrossan Dry Dock and Shipping Co. in 1914, and owned by the New Morecambe Central Pier Co. Ltd., of Bradford, was available for charter. Tucker's took the option and brought her to the Bristol Channel to begin two interesting experiments; the use of a screw steamer in waters where paddle propulsion traditionally reigned supreme, and the provision of a winter service between Cardiff, Weston and Bristol for the first time for many years.

Capt. Jimmy James took command of her and on Saturday 1st. November 1919 she made her first sailing, from Cardiff to Bristol. Two days later she ran a similar trip, this time via Weston with a rail connection to the Bridgewater Fair. Her big day was Christmas Eve when she took 307 passengers to Weston in the morning, and 217 to Bristol in the evening, but in general her passenger numbers were disappointing, sometimes as low as single figures.

An acquaintance of the writer, Mr. Syd Wake, recalls his memories of the **ROBINA** on this winter service. As a boy he was taken by his father on one of her trips to Bristol and remembers that for most of the journey, together with a small number of other passengers, they sat in the saloon around a paraffin stove, trying to keep warm in the bitterly cold weather. His father remarked, "Remember this my boy. I don't think we'll see the like of this again." How right he was!

The **BRITANNIA'S** refit having been completed, she left Harland & Wolff's yard at Govan, Glasgow, under the command of Capt. J. H. Denman, on Friday 19th. December. She called at Kilmun Pier and spent the night at Gourock. After compass adjusting on the following morning she called at Kirn and ran on the measured mile for speed tests until 13.30 when she sailed for Troon to take on coal. Her log book continues:-

"Saturday 20th. December 1919.
18.20   Left Troon
19.50   Passed Ailsa Craig
21.00   Corsewall Point (Stranraer)
23.30   South Rock

Sunday 21st. December 1919.

08.20	Bardsey Island
13.05	South Bishop
14.10	St. Ann's Head
14.45	St. Govan's Head
15.30	Caldey Island
17.05	Mumbles Head
19.20	Nash Point
21.15	Penarth Roads (To anchor)
	NW strong wind, heavy sea.
	Bad coal. About 60/80lbs. steam.

Monday 22nd. December 1919.

05.30	Left Penarth Roads
06.25	Entered River Avon
07.00	Arrived at Bristol
	Entered Basin."

Plans for the refitting of the **ALBION** were abandoned when a survey revealed that the after part of the ship had been twisted by the fire caused by a direct hit during a bombing raid at Dunkirk. Although the ship herself was beyond repair, her engines were still in perfectly good condition and it was proposed to use them in the company's new steamer, then under construction at the Ailsa Shipbuilding Co's yard.

With Capt. J. H. Denman in command, the **ALBION** left Bristol for Troon, where she was to be broken up, on the evening of Wednesday 18th. February 1920, in tow of the local tug **VICTOR**. In Barry Roads the tow was taken over by the tug **STORMCOCK.** At 10.00 next day she put into Milford Haven as the tug had engine trouble, but proceeded at 17.00 only to put back again after encountering heavy weather near the Bishops. She eventually left Milford Haven on Sunday 22nd. February at 06.30, arriving at Troon at 18.00 on the following day.

The **ROBINA** continued her winter service from Cardiff but, by Saturday 13th. March 1920, she had discontinued her Bristol trips and was running to Weston two or three times daily. This she continued to do until Maundy Thursday 1st. April when she was joined by the **LADY EVELYN** and the **LADY MOYRA,** for the Easter weekend. Campbell's brought out the **RAVENSWOOD, GLEN AVON, CAMBRIA, GLEN USK** and **BRITANNIA.**

It was the custom for four or five White Funnel steamers to be put into operation over Easter, most of which would then be withdrawn until Whitsun, when the whole fleet would enter service.

After the cold and wet Easter of 1920 the **LADY MOYRA** was laid up until Thursday 20th. May. The **ROBINA** was also taken out of service for overhaul, leaving the **LADY EVELYN** and the **GLEN AVON** on the Cardiff to Weston ferry, until she rejoined them on Thursday 13th. May, under the command of Capt. Hector McFadyen.

The **LADY EVELYN** very rarely made any trips to Ilfracombe but visited there on Tuesday 18th. May, when she landed a mere 18 passengers. She was scheduled to repeat the trip on the following day but as only 20 passengers turned up, 14 of whom had complimentary passes, the trip was cancelled.

The late Ernest Vivian Tucker was a regular passenger on the White Funnel steamers up to the 1960's and became a good friend of the writer. In conversation over the years Mr. Tucker recalled many memories of his Yellow Funnel days.

One such recollection was of a day in 1920 when such a thick fog developed that hundreds of trippers were stranded at Weston overnight after the **GLEN AVON** and **GLEN USK** were unable to find Birnbeck Pier. The **LADY EVELYN,** however, was more fortunate. As she moved slowly and cautiously, the low water jetty was sighted a few yards from her stern. Having established her position she was then able to make the high water jetty and embark her passengers for Cardiff. The tide was ebbing fast and she reached her home port with little time to spare. It had been a worrying evening for Capt. Bob Case, who had negotiated the Cardiff Roads crowded with vessels at anchor, but it was no less nerve-racking for Mr. Tucker as he waited at the Pier Head, wondering where the steamer was and listening hard in the dense fog for the sound of her paddles.

The low water jetty at Weston had been opened during Whitsun of 1909. It extended about 500ft in a SW direction from Birnbeck Island and enabled the steamers to berth at any state of the tide. However, the prevailing winds and swell from the westward, together with the strong tidal flows and currents, made it a difficult berthing place. Furthermore, if a steamer overshot the jetty she would find herself perilously near the rocks. Consequently, it became most unpopular with the ships' masters and was demolished during the winter of 1921/1922.

Before every season each steamer was inspected by a Board of Trade surveyor and, if found satisfactory, was issued with a certificate which stated the maximum number of passengers that could be carried on the various routes. (See page 66). If the number of passengers exceeded the relevant figure the company was liable to a fine proportionate to the excess. There was an unfortunate incident when Tuckers were fined £40 for carrying 25 passengers over the limit on a return trip from Ilfracombe on the **LADY MOYRA.** It was difficult, however, to be sure of the totals aboard when crowds were pushing to embark and, on a good day, particularly at Weston, more people sometimes waited for the last boat than could be lawfully carried; yet it was hardly a humane gesture to leave them behind. On one occasion, as Mr. Tucker recalled with some amusement, the **LADY EVELYN** was "tipping the scales" when several police officers were seen awaiting her arrival at the Cardiff Pier Head. While they prepared to check the number of passengers descending by the main gangway, the crew slipped out another gangway from the other side of the ship on to the deck of the adjacent steamer. Hastily, a crowd of passengers were hustled across the ship's deck and ashore on to a different pontoon, out of the scrutiny of the counters!

Wednesday was traditionally early closing day in Cardiff and Tucker's ran a few evening cruises up the River Severn by the **LADY MOYRA,** bringing her back from Ilfracombe early to make the run. Mr. Tucker recalled that on one such Wednesday the morning had been dull, with a heavy drizzle, and the **LADY MOYRA** took only a handful of passengers to Ilfracombe. As the day progressed, the weather cleared to give a glorious afternoon and evening. When the **LADY MOYRA** arrived at Cardiff to leave

17

at 17.00 on the cruise, the queue of passengers extended a considerable way from the Pier Head. As it was impossible for her to carry such a large number, one of the pontoon men was detailed to go to a certain point in the queue to inform those behind that there was no hope of boarding the **LADY MOYRA.** They were told that one of the White Funnel steamers was making a cruise to off Burnham-on-Sea, with the result that both steamers were filled to capacity. On the **LADY MOYRA'S** return from Ilfracombe that day, the bar and refreshment room takings amounted to a mere few pounds. On her return from the cruise, however, those takings had increased to over £115; an excellent sum for those days!

In the years before the Great War, one of the few Bristol Channel ports not served by the Campbell fleet was Swansea. This had been the domain of Pockett's Bristol Channel Steam Packet Co. Ltd. However, their sole, remaining passenger steamer, the **BRIGHTON,** had been requisitioned by the Admiralty, in March 1915, for service in the Eastern Mediterranean. At the end of 1919 the Admiralty sold her to Turkish owners, for whom she continued to ply in the Aegean Sea and in the Sea of Marmora until being broken up in 1927. After the war a group of Swansea residents, concerned by the absence of steamer services, approached Alec Campbell with a view to the White Funnel Fleet taking over the Swansea station; a proposal which Alec was only too pleased to accept, having had his eye on it for some time. The company took over Pockett's Wharf, near the South Dock entrance, on the west bank of the River Tawe, with Mr. Arthur Smyth as their agent. Mr. Smyth was a resident of Ilfracombe and had acted as Pockett's agent, at the North Devon resort, before the war.

The **BARRY,** since her arrival at Troon from Devonport on Saturday 27th. September 1919, had been in the hands of the Ailsa Shipbuilding Co. After the completion of her refit she left Troon in time to inaugurate P. & A. Campbell's regular service from Swansea on Whit Saturday 22nd. May 1920, with a day trip to Ilfracombe. The service was taken over, for the rest of the season, by the **GLEN USK** about two weeks later.

The sailings which the company instituted from Swansea and Mumbles were similar to those operated by Pockett's in the pre-war years. Daily trips were made to and from Ilfracombe which were usually extended to either Lundy, Clovelly or Lynmouth and Minehead. The crossing was sometimes routed via Porthcawl or Tenby. Two-hour cruises were run to Porthcawl, around the Scarweather Light Vessel, or along the Gower Coast. Over the years the Swansea to Ilfracombe service proved to be particularly lucrative. The company, in conjunction with the railways, provided combined rail and steamer travel linking all parts of Wales and the Midlands with the West Country.

The Campbell monopoly at Swansea lasted for less than two months. Competition arrived in the form of the 332 gross ton paddle steamer **LADY ROWENA.** This competition constituted very little by way of a threat to the White Funnel Fleet; indeed, the operation of this vessel in the Bristol Channel was particularly haphazard, and on occasions reached almost farcical proportions!

The **LADY ROWENA** had been built by Sam McKnight & Co., at Ayr, in 1891 for the North British Steam Packet Co's services on the River Clyde. From 1903 to 1908 she ran for Italian owners on cruises in the Bay of Naples before being purchased by Richard R. Collard for service on the South Coast of England until returning to the Clyde in 1912. During World War 1 she was used firstly as a fodder carrier, taking animal feed from the East Coast to the French ports. Then, after a period as a troop tender she commenced minesweeping duties, with a further spell in the Mediterranean. After the war she spent the 1919 season on the Humber before her purchase by a syndicate of Swansea residents led by James Henry Jones, Thomas Lewis and Walter Thomas.

The **LADY ROWENA'S** Bristol Channel saga began on Thursday 8th. July 1920 when she left Falmouth for Swansea. Having spent the night of Friday 9th. stormbound at Newlyn, Cornwall, she arrived off Mumbles on Saturday 10th. Capt. Jim Byrne, a Swansea sea pilot described how he brought her into the South Dock:-

> "We were off Mumbles Head in the pilot cutter **BEAUFORT** when we saw this thing coming up. As it was my turn for a ship we went alongside and I boarded her. I asked for the master and one of the hands told me that he was below, in the saloon, so I went down the companionway into the after saloon, which was about a foot deep in water. She had had a very dirty passage around Lands End. The master was dipping up water with a baler and pouring it into a bucket which he then emptied overboard. If I had not stopped him he would be there now!
>
> Before entering the dock the master asked me if we could try a little manoeuvring at the Fairway Buoy. It seemed that they had trouble in reversing the engine; before it could go astern, the engine had to be stopped while a cotter pin was slipped out of the reversing gear, otherwise the slide valve would not operate. Before the cotter pin could be slipped out the engine had to make one extra, complete revolution ahead".

Mr. George Owen remembers his father taking him to see the **LADY ROWENA** lying at the Glasgow Wharf in the South Dock basin. Even though only nine years old he was horrified by her scruffy and unkempt appearance when compared with the far superior Campbell vessels. Her hull was light grey, with the saloon strake and paddle boxes white. Her badly dented funnel was blue, with a deep, black top although this was repainted in a buff colour with a narrow black top for most of her forthcoming season.

She made her first, trial cruise from Swansea on Friday 16th. July with 100 invited guests. On the following day the **GLEN USK** sailed on a morning trip to Ilfracombe and, although unadvertised, the **LADY ROWENA** hovered, like a hungry wolf, to pick up any scraps and make a cruise should the **GLEN USK** leave any passengers behind, but the White Funnel steamer comfortably lifted the lot. Later in the day the **LADY ROWENA** did make a trip, having "pinched" a crowd of passengers waiting for the **GLEN USK'S** afternoon sailing. Her master did not have a pilot's licence and so had to employ a pilot to take her in and out of Swansea. This was fortunate in that it enables Capt. Byrne to take up the story again:

> "As we were coming up to the jetty, on the return to Swansea, I called "Stop", and then "Full astern", but before the engine could go astern the extra revolution forward had to be made, with the result that she ran, like a destroyer, into two mud barges!. There was quite a panic on board, a number of passengers climbing across the barges to get ashore in a hurry. The barges were covered in mud and, as may be imagined, those who disembarked in this manner were sorry objects."

In addition to damaging the barges the **LADY ROWENA** sank two small boats and collided with the quay, badly twisting her stem above the waterline, before she could be pulled up. She was withdrawn from service - an inauspicious start to an eventful season.

On Tuesday 20th. July she was issued with a certificate to carry 534 passengers but this was of no use to her for nearly a month, for on Friday 21st. it was announced that she would leave for Bristol, on the following day, for repairs. Immediately, a writ was issued against her, no doubt for damage to the other vessels in the collision. However, she left Swansea on Saturday 22nd. July and was towed to Bristol where she entered Stothert's Dry Dock.

It was unfortunate that the **LADY ROWENA** sustained her accident on that particular weekend as she would otherwise have found profitable business when King George V and Queen Mary visited Swansea. They arrived in the Royal Yacht **VICTORIA AND ALBERT**, escorted by the Battleships **QUEEN ELIZABETH, BARHAM, MALAYA, VALIANT** and **WARSPITE**, which anchored in Swansea Bay. The **RAVENSWOOD** ran a cruise to accompany the ships along the Gower Coast as they arrived on the evening of Friday 16th. July. On Saturday 17th. and Monday 19th. she ran a series of hourly trips from Swansea and Mumbles to enable passengers to board the warships, before following the visiting fleet down channel on its departure. The **RAVENSWOOD** was also based at Swansea at intervals during that season for the express purpose of "running off" the **LADY ROWENA.**

It was the custom, in those days, for one of the steamers, often the versatile **RAVENSWOOD,** to be based for short periods, at the height of the seasons, at Ilfracombe for the purpose of augmenting the sailings. In 1920, among the trips operated by the **RAVENSWOOD** during one of those spells took place on Tuesday 27th. July when she ran a day trip from Ilfracombe to Bideford. This was the first post-war trip up the River Torridge to the North Devon port and may have been the first ever Campbell visit. Whether or not they called there in the pre-war years is uncertain.

The last of the White Funnel steamers to be refitted after the war were the **WESTWARD HO,** which had entered service from Cardiff, under the command of Capt. Joe Ashford, on Saturday 22nd. May, and the **DEVONIA.** The latter began sailing on Monday 5th. July having undergone a particularly extensive overhaul at Bristol which included a three month period in Stothert's Dry Dock. She immediately took on the longer sailings from Cardiff, via Minehead and Lynmouth, or Porthcawl and Mumbles, to Ilfracombe and beyond. As sister ship to the **LADY MOYRA,** daily tussles for supremacy between the two ships frequently took place on the Ilfracombe run, with the honours fairly equally divided.

On Tuesday 24th. August the **DEVONIA** ran the first post-war trip to Newquay, leaving Cardiff at 07.15, Ilfracombe at 10.15 and arriving at the Cornish resort at 14.30, allowing about two hours ashore. This marathon excursion took place three or four times during the high summers of the 1920's.

The **LADY ROWENA** returned to Swansea on Wednesday 18th. August. The syndicate of her owners found themselves in considerable financial difficulties, but were fortunate enough to be joined by Walter Kenneth David, a colliery agent, who injected further capital into the venture. She was advertised as:-

"Swansea's Own Steamer.
The Magnificent Saloon Steamer Lady Rowena.
Rally up and support local enterprise."

Over the following six weeks she followed a most erratic pattern of sailings, some of which defy logical explanation. For example:-

Tuesday 24th. July 1920.
She carried four passengers from Swansea to Llanelly. 105 passengers then embarked for Tenby but, for reasons unknown, they returned from Tenby to Llanelly by train.

Tuesday 31st. August 1920.
She ran light from Swansea to Llanelly where a crowd of about 500 passengers embarked for Tenby. Only 300 of those passengers returned in her. She could not make Llanelly on the return trip, for tidal reasons, and returned to Swansea where, having again missed the tide, her passengers had to disembark by climbing an iron rung quay wall ladder in the early hours of the morning.

Wednesday 1st. September 1920.
Her one and only scheduled trip to Lundy was cancelled when only three intending passengers turned up.

Saturday 4th. September 1920.
She sailed light from Swansea to Llanelly, where she lay idle for the following two days, and then sent a message to Swansea for four tons of coal to be delivered urgently, by road. She returned, light again, to Swansea, on the 6th. where she completed bunkering, and on the 7th. went to Llanelly, only to return again on the same day without carrying passengers in either direction!

Thursday 9th. September 1920.
Outwardly, things were going well. She had 201 passengers aboard for her afternoon cruise, but the records reveal that of this number only 25 of them were fare paying; the rest were travelling on advertisers free passes.

Her single cylinder, diagonal engine generated a very slow speed. Mr. Owen recalls that on one Saturday she left Swansea for Ilfracombe, followed about half an hour later by the **GLEN USK,** bound for the same destination. The latter passed her in mid-channel, landed at Ilfracombe and was on her way back to Swansea when she met the **LADY ROWENA** again, still making her plodding progress to North Devon.

In a flurry of activity she made a number of successful cruises towards the end of September, but it was too late. On Thursday 30th her crew were paid off and she was laid up; her Bristol Channel venture had been a disaster!. In March of the following year she was chartered to Mr. F. C. Deering for service from Brighton and left Swansea for the Sussex resort on Tuesday 5th. July 1921. She was, however, withdrawn from service on the south coast in September 1921 and was eventually broken up in November 1922.

Meanwhile, in the summer of 1920, the White Funnel steamers ran without a hitch, until Monday 20th. September, when the **CAMBRIA,** suffered a major breakdown. She was running a day trip from Cardiff to Minehead, Lynmouth, Ilfracombe and Clovelly when, off Lynmouth, a loud bang was heard in the port paddle box. Investigation showed that the paddle shaft had broken at the outside bearing and that the paddle wheel had dropped by about two feet. The **GLEN USK,** on her way from Swansea to Ilfracombe, Lynmouth and Minehead, went alongside the **CAMBRIA** and embarked her passengers, returning with them to Ilfracombe. The Cardiff tugs **WELSH ROSE** and **ASSISTANCE** arrived at the **CAMBRIA'S** position at 16.15 and proceeded to tow her to Bristol, where she arrived at 00.20 next day, to lay up for the winter, during which repairs were effected.

Since their return from war service the **GLEN ROSA** and the **WAVERLEY** had been laid up in Bristol. The 43 year old **GLEN ROSA** was a much travelled steamer, having served on the Clyde, the Thames and the South Coast, before being purchased by Alec Campbell on his own account in 1897. In the following year he sold her to the limited company and she was instrumental in their expansion on the South Coast, firstly at Southampton and later at Brighton.

The **WAVERLEY,** of 1885, was the first White Funnel steamer to run in the Bristol Channel when she came south from Scotland on charter in 1887. She began the Campbell brothers own operations from Bristol in the following season and it was the **WAVERLEY** which established the company's reputation and laid the foundations of the success of the White Funnel Fleet.

On Friday 1st. October, under the supervision of Capt. Allan Livingstone, they were towed up the Floating Harbour, the **GLEN ROSA** to Gas House Point and the **WAVERLEY** to Great Western Point, where they were broken up.

The **ROBINA** had experienced a fairly trouble free season. She had been almost exclusively on the Cardiff to Weston ferry and finished her sailings on Saturday 25th. September. The steamers never ran on Sundays in those days but there was an exception, recalled by Mr. Vivian Tucker. It was the company's outing, taken by the **ROBINA** after she had finished her season, possibly on Sunday 26th. September. It was her one and only trip to Ilfracombe, quite a spontaneous affair and unadvertised. This was to be the end of the **ROBINA'S** Bristol Channel career, she was returned to her owners soon after.

Tucker's ended their season with the **LADY EVELYN** making her last sailing on Monday 4th. October. To that date the Yellow Funnel Fleet had landed 142,086 passengers at Weston during the wet and stormy season, while the larger Campbell fleet had landed 283,000. The **LADY EVELYN** left Cardiff to lay up at Newport on Thursday 14th. October.

The **LADY MOYRA** had made her last service run on Monday 27th. September but ran a special charter trip, with just 19 passengers, to Milford Haven on Wednesday 13th. October. She called at Ilfracombe on the way to land a number of the party, including Mr. Reg. Tucker, who were on their way to Bideford to attend the launching of one of

Messrs. Hansen's steamers, the **HUBBASTONE**. The **LADY MOYRA** left Milford Haven on Friday 15th. October and entered the King's Dock, Swansea, for the winter.

After the season had ended the **BRITANNIA** was re-boilered. She left Bristol, with Capt. Dan Taylor in command, at 08.00 on Thursday 14th. October and, after a stop at Greenock, berthed at Bridge Wharf opposite the Broomielaw Quay, Glasgow, on the morning of Friday 15th. On the following Monday she moved to the yard of A & J. Inglis at Pointhouse where, over the next few weeks, the new boiler was installed, the old one being retained for renovation and further use. On Monday 8th. December she was moved to Bowling Harbour to lay up for the winter.

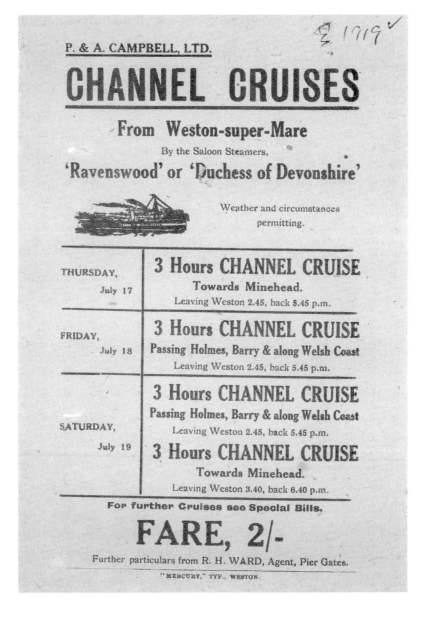

The DUCHESS OF DEVONSHIRE arriving at Weston during her period on charter to P. & A. Campbell Ltd., 1917/1919. (CCC)

The GLEN AVON at Troon. July 1919. Her post-war refit has been completed and she will shortly return to the Bristol Channel. (CCC)

Date 16th August 1919

STEAMER.	Time Arrived.	Time of Departure.	No Landed.	No. Left on Board.	No Embarked.	DESTINATION.
Duchess	9.19	9.28	765		179	
L/Q	9.58	10.10	625		174	
G Avon	10.15	10.25	847		148	
Ravenswood	11.5	11.20	251	578	115	Minehead & I Combe
Duchess	11.26	11.40	507		500	
L/Q	12.2	12.16	649		529	
G Avon	12.20	12.45	484		661	
Duchess	1.58	2.35	539	X	163	Crew
G Avon	2.50	3.5	543	I	90	"
L/Q	3.7	3.28	661	O	145	"
Duchess	5.11	6.34	163		400	
L/Q	5.28	6.10	145	O	600	
G Avon	5.40	6.10	90	I	1075	
Ravenswood	8.32	8.38	108		192	
G Avon	8.41	8.53	174		831	
L/Q	8.58	9.12	238		556	
Duchess	9.16	9.21	24		76	
L/M		to come for about 150.				

```
                    TOTAL
            DUCHESS  1335 - 1105
            G. AVON  2048 - 2655
                     3383   3460

            EVELYN   2173 - 1859
            MOYRA      -     150
                     2173 - 2009
```

Private The Police commenced to count passengers
out here today and started with G Avon @ 12.20
I immediately informed Cardiff but too late to
do any good for Duchess. I took the bull by the horns
and informed Sergt. that she had about 60 more than
she ought and asked him to give me a chance, as a
matter of fact she had 119 over, he concurred &
when he finished informed me she had 418.
Had it been any other ——— I should have failed.
Great care must be exercised for some little time

The company's agents sent a daily return to the head office at Bristol giving full details of the number of passengers who embarked and disembarked at their port of call. Added to the above return from the Weston agent, is an interesting footnote

25

The LADY EVELYN off Portishead. The all-yellow funnel indicates her first Bristol Channel season –1919. (CCC).

The LADY MOYRA brings a full complement of passengers to board the Battle Cruiser LION in Swansea Bay. Thursday 11th September 1919. The narrow black tops of her funnels were a feature of 1919 only. (CCC)

The tranquillity of a summer evening cruise. The LADY EVELYN leaving Cardiff in 1920. During that year all the yellow funnels appeared with deep black tops. (CCC)

Aboard the RAVENSWOOD arriving alongside the Battleship QUEEN ELIZABETH in Swansea Bay. July 1920. (CCC)

The LADY MOYRA arrives at Porthcawl, 1920. The DEVONIA waits offshore. (CCC)

The DEVONIA berths at the breakwater, Porthcawl. 1920. (CCC)

The first White Funnel sailing from Swansea. The BARRY leaves Pockett's Wharf for Ilfracombe on the morning of Whit Saturday 22nd. May 1920. (CCC)

Photographs of the Yellow Funnel steamers are few and the rarity of this view compensates for its poor quality. The LADY MOYRA lies alongside the GLEN USK and RAVENSWOOD at the Stone Bench, Ilfracombe, during the wet and windy summer of 1920. (CCC)

P. & A. CAMPBELL LTD.

Sailings from Cardiff by Magnificent Saloon Steamers of the
WHITE FUNNEL FLEET

Britannia, Cambria, Westward Ho! Devonia, Barry, Glen Usk, Glen Avon, Ravenswood, &c.
(Weather and circumstances permitting)

Friday, **Sept. 24th** Note Alterations	**WESTON** Leave Cardiff 8.30 am, 12.50, 2.0, 4.0, 6.0 pm Leave Weston 12.45, 2.45, 4.45 7.15 7.35 pm **MINEHEAD (via WESTON)** Leave Cardiff 12.50 pm Return Minehead 6.0 pm **CLEVEDON and BRISTOL** Leave Cardiff 1.15 pm Return Bristol 4.0 pm and 6 30 pm Clevedon 7.30 pm Single Trip to ILFRACOMBE (calling off LYNMOUTH) Leave Cardiff 6.0 pm Note.—A Steamer leaves Ilfracombe at 10.15 am for Cardiff (calling off Lynmouth)
Saturday, **Sept 25th** Note Alterations	**WESTON** Leave Cardiff 9.30, am, 1.50, 2.40, 3.50, 5.45, 7.0, 7.30 pm Leave Weston 1.20, 2.40, 3.25, 4.35, 6.30, 8.0, 8.30 pm **ILFRACOMBE (calling off LYNMOUTH)** Leave Cardiff 9.15 am Return Ilfracombe 4.30 pm **Afternoon Trip to BRISTOL** Leave Cardiff 2.15 pm Return Bristol 7.15 pm **Evening Trip to CLEVEDON and BRISTOL** Leave Cardiff 5.0 pm Clevedon 7.15 pm Clevedon 8.30 pm Return Fares: Clevedon 2/6, Bristol 3/- Note.—A Steamer leaves Bristol at 7.20 am for Cardiff. Note.—A Steamer leaves Ilfracombe at 11.15 am (calling off Lynmouth) for Cardiff
Monday, **Sept. 27th** Note Alterations	**WESTON** Leave Cardiff 8.0, 9.40 am, 2.30, 3.15, 5.15, 7.5 pm Leave Weston 8.45 am, 1.45, 4.0, 6.0, 8.0 8.20 pm **ILFRACOMBE (calling off LYNMOUTH)** Leave Cardiff 9.30 am Return Ilfracombe 4.0 pm **Afternoon Trip to BRISTOL** Leave Cardiff 2.40 pm Return Bristol 7.30 pm **Afternoon Trip to MINEHEAD (via Weston)** Leave Cardiff 2.30 pm Return Minehead 6.45 pm Return Fare, 5/- **BY REQUEST. Special Evening Cruise to off BURNHAM passing THE HOLMES** **and BREAN DOWN** Leave Cardiff 6.30 pm Back about 9.15 pm Fare 2s.
Tuesday, **Sept. 28th**	**WESTON** Leave Cardiff 8.30, 10.0 am, 3 20, 4.0, 5.20, 7.15 pm Leave Weston 9.15 am, 2.45, 4.10, 6.0, 7.45 8.0 pm **ILFRACOMBE (calling off LYNMOUTH)** Leave Cardiff 10.5 am Return Ilfracombe 2.45 pm ━━━ **SPECIAL EXCURSION! 21st ANNUAL CHARITY TRIP** In aid of King Edward VII. and Seamen's Hospitals **BRISTOL** Leave Cardiff 3.30 pm Return Bristol 8.30 pm Return Fare 3/- **BAND of the Glamorgan Royal Garrison Artillery (T.)** (by kind permission of Major A. P. Carey Thomas, T.D., and Officers), will give selections on board during the above Trip. Conductor: Bandmaster T. J. O'Leary. Or to **WESTON** Leave Cardiff 4.0 pm Return Weston 6.0, 7.45, or 8.0 pm Return Fare, 3/- Passes are not available for the above trips. ━━━ Single Trip to CLEVEDON & BRISTOL Leave Cardiff 5.30 pm Note.—A Steamer leaves Bristol at 8.0 am, Clevedon at 8.50 am, for Cardiff
Wednesday **Sept. 29th**	**WESTON** Leave Cardiff 9.0, 10.30 am, 4.15, 5.15, 6.15, 7.15 pm Leave Weston 9.45 am, 3.45, 5.0, 6.0, 8.0, 8.15 pm **ILFRACOMBE (calling off Lynmouth)** Leave Cardiff 9.30 am Return Ilfracombe 4.0 pm **Evening Trip to WESTON** (allowing 2 hours on shore) Leave Cardiff 5.15 pm Return Weston 8.15 pm Fare 2/6 **Special Evening Cruise passing Barry Island, Roos Point and Breaksea Lightship** Leave Cardiff 6.30 pm Back about 9.30 pm Fare 2s.
Thursday, **Sept. 30th**	**WESTON** Leave Cardiff 9.40, 11.0 am, 5.0, 6.0, 7.0, 7.45 pm Leave Weston 10.25 am, 4.15, 5.45, 6.45, 8.15, 8.30 pm **ILFRACOMBE (calling off Lynmouth)** Leave Cardiff 9.30 am Return Ilfracombe 4.0 pm **Evening Trip to WESTON** (allowing 2½ hours on shore) Leave Cardiff 5.0 pm Return Weston 8.30 pm Fare 2/6 Single Trip to BRISTOL Leave Cardiff 6.30 pm
Friday, **Oct. 1st**	**WESTON** Leave Cardiff 9.40, 11.45 am 5.15 pm Leave Weston 10.25 am, 4.0, 7.15 pm **ILFRACOMBE (calling off LYNMOUTH)** Leave Cardiff 10.20 am Return Ilfracombe 4.0 pm Single Trip to BRISTOL Leave Cardiff 6.30 pm Note.—A Steamer leaves Bristol at 8.30 am for Cardiff
Saturday, **Oct. 2nd**	**WESTON** Leave Cardiff 9.30, 10.30, 11.30 am, 12 40, 5.45 pm Leave Weston 10.15, 11.15 am, 4.30, 6 30, 7.15 pm **ILFRACOMBE (calling off LYNMOUTH)** Leave Cardiff 10.30 am Return Ilfracombe 4.30 pm **CLEVEDON (via Weston)** Leave Cardiff 12.40 pm Return Clevedon 5.40 pm Single Trip to BRISTOL Leave Cardiff 7.0 pm Note.—A Steamer leaves Bristol at 8 30 am for Cardiff

FARES—

	Single	Day Return	Tourist			Single	Day Return
CLEVEDON	3s.	4s.	-	**WESTON**		3s.	4s.
BRISTOL	3s.	4s. 6d.	-	" at 5.0 p.m. and after			
MINEHEAD or WATCHET	4s. 6d.	6s.	3s.	(Saturdays excepted)		2s.6d.	2s.6d.
LYNMOUTH & ILFRACOMBE	6s.	7s.6d.	10s.	" Tourist			5s.

Children under 12 years of age, half-fare. Dogs, Bicycles, Prams and Mail Carts (at Owner's risk) 2s. each way.
Lynmouth Fares do not include landing and embarking. Steamer calls off Lynmouth to-and-fro and leaves Lynmouth 35 minutes after leaving Ilfracombe.
The Company cannot convey Motor Cycles or Side Cars.   The Steamers will not call at Penarth.
The Company do not hold themselves responsible to sail at the advertised times, but will use every endeavour to carry out the sailings. A reasonable quantity
of luggage carried at Passengers own risk. Passengers are requested to label same.

For further particulars, etc., apply to WM. GUY, Agent, 1, Stuart Street, Cardiff;
T. COOK & SON, 28, High Street, Cardiff; or
P. & A. CAMPBELL, Ltd., Cumberland Basin, Bristol.

Telegrams: "RAVENSWOOD, CARDIFF." "WARD. PIER, WESTON." "RAVENSWOOD," BRISTOL."
Telephone: CARDIFF 723. WESTON 44. BRISTOL 3112.

Dates, Ltd., Printers, Docks, Cardiff.

Cardiff Timetable for 1920.

The LADY ROWENA arriving at Ilfracombe in 1920. (CCC)

The LADY MOYRA at Riverside Wharf, Swansea, in 1920. (CCC)

The BRITANNIA at the yard of A. & J. Inglis, Pointhouse, Glasgow, during her re-boilering.
November/December 1920. (CCC)

The ALBION at Troon. 1920. (CCC)

Chapter 2 – 1921/1924

The **LADY EVELYN** was due to commence running on Maundy Thursday 24th. March 1921, but owing to unforseen circumstances, she did not sail. Reginald Tucker, being a particularly superstitious man, would not commence the season on a Friday, so it was not until Saturday 26th. March that she made her first trip.

The **GLEN AVON** commenced her season on Maundy Thursday and was joined, for a few days, by the **CAMBRIA** and **RAVENSWOOD.**

The summer of 1921 brought exceptionally fine weather, the best for many years, but the coastal passenger trade, in general, was adversely affected by the coal miners strike which began on Friday 1st. April and continued until the end of June.

The miners had welcomed the wartime take over of the mines by the government. However, now that they were handed back to their owners, the government refusing to nationalise them, the miners went on strike in protest. A state of emergency was declared, and rationing of supplies began on Sunday 3rd. April.

After Easter the only steamers in service were the **LADY EVELYN** and the **GLEN AVON** which ran a limited schedule of sailings between Cardiff and Weston.

The **BRITANNIA,** following her re-boilering, was stranded in Scotland because of the strike. She had run a trial trip on Thursday 5th. May and performed well, the Memorandum book recording:- "Speed 19¼ knots, ample steam." She eventually left Greenock for Bristol on Wednesday 8th. June.

The **WESTWARD HO** also sailed north for re-boilering by A. & J. Inglis, leaving Bristol on Wednesday 22nd. June and arriving back on Monday 11th. July. She was fitted with the haystack boiler removed from the **BRITANNIA** in the previous year which had been re-floored and re-tubed.

The strike ended on Tuesday 28th. June, when the government agreed to subsidise the coal industry. The miners returned to work during the following week and gradually coal supplies returned to normal.

Rainfall on Saturday 25th. June marked the end of a 100 day drought but more, long spells of fine weather were to follow. Although passenger figures had been high on the limited schedule of sailings, it was frustrating to consider how much revenue had been lost in the early months of the season because of the shortage of coal and the consequent late start of most of the steamers.

The **LADY MOYRA** began service on Wednesday 6th. July but it was not until Monday 18th. that all the Campbell steamers were in operation. Five of them - **BRITANNIA, CAMBRIA, DEVONIA, RAVENSWOOD** and **GLEN USK** had been equipped with Marconi Radio installations and short masts, known as "jiggers", on their after decks, with spreaders to carry the aerials to their foremasts.

That year also brought the resumption of the occasional pre-war sailings to Porlock, on the Somerset coast. Both the **WESTWARD HO** and **RAVENSWOOD** called there, the passengers being landed in small boats.

Towards the end of the season the **WESTWARD HO** was involved in an unfortunate accident. On the evening of Friday 30th. September she was returning from Bristol to Cardiff when, having just passed the English and Welsh Grounds Light Vessel, she collided with the schooner **MARGARET WEST,** Capt. Joe Ashford mistaking her anchor light (on the foremast) for the stern light of a steamer. The schooner's bowsprit hit the port paddle box, rebounded and then ran along the rails of the after promenade deck, sweeping three teenage girls into the sea. They were quickly rescued by boats from both vessels; one had sustained a broken leg but the others were little more than bruised and badly shaken. A fourth, male passenger had been swept on to the schooner's deck but received only minor injuries. The **WESTWARD HO** was withdrawn from service next day and returned to Bristol for repairs and to lay up for the winter.

The **LADY MOYRA** had spent most of the season running between Cardiff, Weston and Barry, making only a few trips down channel. Both companies were seriously affected by the miners strike but Tucker's had been hit harder after Campbell's had bought up the major share of available coal stocks. Tucker's were therefore seeking ways of improving their deteriorating financial situation when their attention was drawn to the problems of the Minehead Pier Company.

An extraordinary meeting of that company had been held on Tuesday 5th. July 1921 to consider its financial position which:-

> "...in consequence of the war and, having regard to further expenditure required in the near future, had been seriously prejudiced."

The Chairman explained that in addition to the lack of revenue from the steamers during the war years, as soon as the pier re-opened the company was faced with extensive costs of labour and materials. During the war very little money had been spent on the pier and there had been considerable deterioration especially of the landing stage. On top of the war came the coal strike and further loss of revenue. In conclusion a resolution was passed that:-

> "It has been proved to the satisfaction of this meeting that the company cannot, by reason of its liabilities, continue its business and accordingly the company should be wound up voluntarily."

The chairman then stated that arrangements would be put in hand for the pier to be sold by auction. The "West Somerset Free Press" later reported:-

> "The 20 year old pier at Minehead was duly offered for sale by auction at the Plume of Feathers Hotel on Friday 22nd. July 1921. After fairly brisk bidding it was knocked down to Mr. R. Tucker of Messrs. W. H. Tucker & Co. Ltd., Cardiff, owners of the Yellow Funnel Fleet, the purchase price being £2550".

The tying up of this capital, the loss of revenue because of the coal strike and three seasons competing with the formidable opposition of the larger, Campbell fleet was more than the company could sustain and the days of the Yellow Funnel Fleet were drawing to a close.

As a final gesture of defiance, on the evening of Saturday 17th. September, the **LADY EVELYN** attempted to reach Weston Pier first by cutting across the bows of the **BARRY.** There was a collision and the latter vessel received a badly damaged paddle box resulting in her withdrawal from service, for the winter, on the following day.

The **LADY MOYRA** had entered the King's Dock, Swansea, on Saturday 1st. October to lay up. The **LADY EVELYN** made her last trips to Weston on the same day and joined the **LADY MOYRA** in Swansea on Wednesday 5th. October. At Campbell's board meeting in October 1921 it was reported that Tucker's had failed to complete their recent purchase of Minehead Pier. Campbell's solicitors had therefore re-opened negotiations and it was proposed and seconded that they should purchase the pier.

The board also heard Capt. Peter's report on his meeting with Mr. E. V. Tucker at which he was informed that W. H. Tucker & Co. Ltd. were prepared to sell the **LADY MOYRA** and the **LADY EVELYN** for £50,000. Capt. Peter remained non-committal in replying to this proposal, simply advising them that he could not recommend the directors to offer more than £20,000 for the two vessels.

On Thursday 27th. October a meeting of the creditors of the Yellow Funnel Fleet took place at the Imperial Hotel, Cardiff, and the company went into liquidation. The opposition was over!

The long awaited, new White Funnel steamer appeared in 1922. She was launched at the Ailsa Shipbuilding Co's yard at Troon by Mrs. Alec Campbell on Tuesday 14th. February and named **GLEN GOWER.**

She had been ordered in October 1919 and her keel was laid on 13th. February 1920. Her building had been a long process because of a shortage of steel following the war and a series of shipyard strikes. In fact, after the laying of her keel, she remained untouched for a year. However, she was quickly fitted out, the **ALBION'S** engines were installed and she ran a builders trial on Friday 24th. March. The memorandum book records:-

> "Satisfactory trial. Revs 52. Boiler pressure 140. Southerly breeze. Moderate sea. Very comfortable ship."

Her official trials took place in the Firth of Clyde on Wednesday 24th. May 1922 and were most satisfactory. Capt. Dan Taylor was in command and Peter and Alec were aboard, the latter wiring to the office at Bristol:

> "Good trial speed in strong wind - 17½ knots."

Her first sailing after her trials was from Troon to Kilmun, carrying the **GLEN AVON'S** original mast, which had been replaced during her post-war refit. Alec wanted to set it up as a flagstaff at his home in Kilmun but it was found to be partially rotten and unsuitable for the purpose. After being laid aside for some years the sound portion became a cargo derrick on Kilmun Pier.

The **GLEN GOWER** sailed from Troon at 05.10 on Thursday 25th. May and arrived at Hotwells Landing Stage, Bristol, at 06.50 on the following day, after a "Good trip around".

The "Bristol Channel Guide", the company's official handbook, described the new steamer:-

"In several respects, both in design and construction, she is of a similar type to the "Glen Usk". The "Glen Gower" has been built throughout as a cross-channel steamer for a No.2 certificate (which includes wireless telegraphy) which will enable her to ply anywhere in the United Kingdom. In order to secure her safety, and render her practically unsinkable, the vessel has been built entirely of steel, and divided into watertight compartments, the scantlings of which are in accordance with the latest recommendations of the Bulkhead Committee, rendering it possible for the vessel to float with even two compartments in free communication with the sea.

The "Glen Gower" is fitted with a pair of compound diagonal engines and steam is supplied by a double ended marine boiler of improved type, with a working pressure sufficient for driving the vessel at full speed with modified forced draught...

The carrying capacity of the new steamer is about 1250 passengers. She is upholstered, furnished and decorated in the most tasteful and luxurious manner, no expense having been spared to secure a maximum of comfort and safety for her passengers. There is a complete installation of electric light and the general accommodation is of a very superior description".

Her maiden trip took place on Friday 2nd. June, when she left Bristol at 12.30 and sailed direct to Ilfracombe, arriving at 16.27, with 68 passengers, including Capt.Peter. She sailed light to Swansea that evening in readiness to begin her season on the following morning, Whit Saturday, under the command of Capt. Duncan Smith.

A few weeks after entering service she went to the assistance of the **CAMBRIA.** While the latter was backing out of Ilfracombe, on the afternoon of Thursday 22nd. June, a link in her steering chain snapped. The **GLEN GOWER** towed her into the harbour, where she was repaired overnight.

The summer of 1922 began with mainly warm, sunny weather but from Friday 23rd. June it became predominantly wet and windy. The **GLEN GOWER** experienced her first rough crossing to Ilfracombe on Saturday 24th. June, when Capt. Smith reported to the Bristol office:-

"Glen Gower - very fine seaboat. Behaved splendidly and shipped no water".

On Thursday 6th. July the **BRITANNIA** sailed from Avonmouth and Barry to Ilfracombe in a WNW gale. In mid-channel she was struck by a number of exceptionally heavy seas which stove in several plates of the starboard wing house and flattened a ventilator on the foredeck. She reached Ilfracombe but Capt. Taylor did not proceed to Clovelly as scheduled. The wild conditions continued for a few days and on Saturday 8th. July the **GLEN GOWER** left Swansea at 15.20 to battle through a westerly gale, arriving at Ilfracombe at 19.00, two hours late, having been slowed down to half speed all the way across! Mr. Owen states:

"I watched her leaving that afternoon. She cleared Mumbles Head and met the full force of the terrible weather. As she topped the crests of the mountainous seas I could see daylight under her keel as far back as the bridge".

In her first season the **GLEN GOWER** proved, as she was destined to do on many occasions during her career, that she could well withstand the onslaught of massive seas which the Atlantic Ocean hurled into the Bristol Channel.

Despite the appalling weather, a variety of interesting trips took place that year. On Tuesday 25th. July the **BARRY** ran the ever popular day trip from Ilfracombe to Clovelly, with a "Grand Sea Cruise to off Tintagel Castle, Cornwall". She arrived back at Ilfracombe in time to leave again at 17.00 on an evening trip to Bideford, with a cruise in the River Torridge. The **WESTWARD HO** ran a couple of day trips from Sharpness to Ilfracombe, and there was a series of calls at Watchet by both the **RAVENSWOOD** and the **GLEN AVON**.

On the evening of Saturday 19th. September the **DEVONIA,** returning from Ilfracombe and Cardiff to Bristol, collided with the outward bound steamer, **CITY OF AMIENS,** in the River Avon, just underneath the Clifton Suspension Bridge. The **DEVONIA'S** port paddle box was damaged and the subsequent enquiry found her to be at fault. The company was required to pay £512 10s in settlement of the claim by the owners of the **CITY OF AMIENS.**

Following the demise of the Yellow Funnel Fleet, the **LADY EVELYN** and the **LADY MOYRA** had remained in the King's Dock, Swansea, until their purchase by P. & A. Campbell Ltd. They left for refitting at Bristol on Thursday 6th. July, the **LADY EVELYN** under her own steam, and the **LADY MOYRA** in tow of the tugs **BELLE** and **DEERHOUND.** The change of ownership was registered on Thursday 3rd. August 1922.

It would appear that the company did not really want the ships but the purchase price of £24,498 was too tempting. No doubt they were expecting to re-sell them at a profit, but no such sale took place. This speculation has arisen from a remark made by Capt. Alec at the board meeting on Tuesday 3rd. April 1923 when he stated that there were "no probable buyers for the Lady Moyra and Lady Evelyn". Consequently, he proposed to send two steamers to re-open the South Coast services from Brighton at Whitsun.

In fact, three steamers were detailed to resume the Sussex Coast sailings in 1923, the **DEVONIA,** the **LADY EVELYN,** (re-named **BRIGHTON BELLE**), and the **RAVENSWOOD.** The first two left Bristol on the same day. The **DEVONIA** was one of the fastest steamers of the fleet and the **BRIGHTON BELLE** one of the slowest, a fact illustrated by a comparison of their timings for the round trip to Newhaven.

Wednesday 16th. May 1923

BRIGHTON BELLE. (Capt. B. W. Hawken) **DEVONIA.** (Capt. W. A. Couves)
06.15. Left Bristol.(Cumberland Basin) 08.05. Left Bristol Pontoon.
11.00. Foreland Point. 10.17. Left Cardiff.
 13.18. Passed Ilfracombe.
14.20. Brighton Belle was overtaken by Devonia in Bideford Bay
20.55. Trevose Head. 20.43. Passed the Longships.

Weather: NW wind. Sleet. Very cold

Thursday 17th. May 1923

01.50. Passed the Longships.	
07.15. Passed Eddystone.	01.00. Passed Eddystone.
09.15. Passed Start Point.	02.50. Passed Start Point.
19.00. Passed St. Catherine's Point.	09.05. Passed St. Catherine's Point.
23.25. Berthed at Newhaven.	11.50. Arrived at West Pier,
(No passengers carried)	Brighton.
	(Approx 50 passengers
	disembarked).
	13.14. Left Brighton.
	14.00. Arrived at Newhaven.

The two steamers re-opened the South Coast sailings on the following Saturday, with the **DEVONIA** making the first post-war trip to Boulogne on Tuesday 22nd. May 1923.

In the Bristol Channel, the **GLEN GOWER** made a record sailing. Capt. Smith reported that, on Thursday 7th. June, she sailed from Mumbles Head to Ilfracombe in 1 hour 16 minutes. She made 51 revs. per minute all the way across, which gave her a speed of 17.3 knots. The sea was calm but she had a slight list to port, because of the balance of coal in her bunkers. Capt. Smith added:-

"I am quite confident that she could have done it two minutes faster if she had been on an even keel".

She had, in fact, sailed from Ilfracombe to Mumbles in 1 hour 17 minutes in 1922. These are reputed to have been the fastest crossings and have never been equalled by any other paddle steamer. The timings could, no doubt, have been bettered by a number of the White Funnel steamers but the fuel consumption would have been particularly high and such sailings would have been totally uneconomical.

The **LADY MOYRA,** resplendent in Campbell's colours, left Bristol for compass adjusting and a trial trip to Ilfracombe on Tuesday 3rd. July. For her first few days in service she was commanded by Capt. Peter Campbell, no doubt interested to see for himself how his new acquisition performed. She sailed, light, from Bristol to Briton Ferry on Friday 13th. July in readiness for a charter trip to Weston on the following day. The trip had to be re-scheduled at the last moment, when thick fog shrouded the channel and Capt. Peter considered it safer to take the charter party across to Ilfracombe rather than negotiate the busy shipping lanes up and down the channel.

To augment the sailings of the **DEVONIA** and the **BRIGHTON BELLE** it was decided to send the **RAVENSWOOD** to the South Coast for the height of the season. After running for the early part of the summer in the Bristol Channel she left Barry, light, at 06.00 on Sunday 29th. July, passed the Lizard at 19.30 and arrived at Newhaven at 13.49 on the following day, giving her an average speed of 11¼ knots for the journey. She began sailing on the following Wednesday, making her first, post-war crossing to Boulogne on Monday 13th. August.

The **LADY MOYRA'S** first White Funnel season, had progressed well, but ended in disaster. On Wednesday 22nd. August she was scheduled to run a day trip from Cardiff to Lynmouth, Ilfracombe and Newquay, but had proceeded no further than Ilfracombe because of the appalling weather. She spent the day at the pier and left Ilfracombe, as scheduled, at 22.00. She backed out slowly into the oncoming swell but her stern fell into a deep trough and she was "pooped" by the following massive sea, which washed over her after deck. The force of the water snapped her steering chain, twisted the rudder post and damaged the rudder itself, rendering her immobile and at the mercy of the violent weather. She dropped anchor but the wild conditions prevented it from holding and she began to drift up channel. The **BARRY,** on an afternoon trip from Cardiff, put out from Ilfracombe and took her in tow to more sheltered water, off Combe Martin, where she was able to anchor. The **BARRY** then ran up channel and contacted the tugs **WHITE ROSE** and **WILD ROSE** which succeeded in reaching the **LADY MOYRA** in the early hours of the following morning. They took her in tow to Barry, where she arrived at 12.30 on Thursday 23rd. August to discharge her weary passengers. She arrived in Bristol that evening and subsequently entered Stothert's Dry Dock for repairs, which included the fitting of a new rudder.

A week later, the **RAVENSWOOD** was caught in a gale while returning from Folkestone to Brighton. She encountered very heavy seas, causing her to cancel her landings at Hastings and Eastbourne. Her master, Capt. Frank Weeks, decided not to venture west of Beachy Head and anchored for the night off Eastbourne. By the early hours of the following morning the weather moderated sufficiently for her to land her passengers.

During late September, stormy weather once again caused widespread disruption to sailings. On Thursday 20th. the **WESTWARD HO** sailed from Avonmouth and Barry, bound for Lynmouth and Ilfracombe. The memorandum book records:-

> "One hour out of Barry, struck a heavy sea - slowed to fix deck seats. On ringing "Full Ahead" again heard sudden noise in paddle box. Ascertained one float broken off and crashed into a second float, carrying that away also. Hoisted sail and put about".

Off the Culver Sands she met the **BARRY,** on her way from Cardiff and Weston to Minehead, which towed her to off Sully Island, where the tugs **WHITE ROSE** and **WILD ROSE** took over and towed her to Penarth Roads. In the meantime the **BARRY** returned to Cardiff, having terminated her Minehead trip, landed her 226 passengers, then went out again to take the 79 passengers off the **WESTWARD HO.**

The above entry states "Hoisted sail". It was a Board of Trade requirement that the steamers should carry two sails on their foremasts, a jib forward and a trysail abaft, for the purpose of assisting the manoeuvring of the vessel in case of a complete engine breakdown. The trysail was the more useful and was sometimes used to prevent excessive "yawing", (ie being pushed from side to side in a heavy, following sea) as on the above occasion, but for most of the time the sails remained furled in their canvas covers.

The late Ernest Dumbleton told of a trip he made in the **BRITANNIA** during the 1920's when, contrary to her usual practice, the ship was running very sluggishly. The trouble appeared to be a supply of poor quality coal which had been bunkered the night before. Between Ilfracombe and Tenby Capt. Taylor had had enough!. He stopped the ship and ordered the firemen to jettison the bad coal until they reached the better quality fuel which he knew lay underneath. The fresh wind and lively sea caused her to roll considerably, making the operation difficult. He therefore had the trysail hoisted to keep the ship's head into the wind to steady her while the firemen emptied the coal into the sea. After reaching the better quality coal, the **BRITANNIA'S** performance improved considerably.

On the day following the **WESTWARD HO'S** accident, the **CAMBRIA** was taking a similar trip from Avonmouth and Barry to Lynmouth and Ilfracombe. To quote the memorandum book again:-

> "About one hour out of Barry, going dead slow, sea carried away foredeck ventilators, stove in wooden panel in forward companionway and another in forward end of chartroom. Put back to Barry."

The **DEVONIA'S** final departure of the season from Boulogne on Sunday 30th.September was accompanied by events worthy of a Buster Keaton film. The "Western Daily Press" reported the details:-

> "As the Bristol pleasure steamer Devonia was leaving Boulogne Harbour after having made her last trip there for the season, five belated passengers made a thrilling dash to overtake her.
>
> The quayside was thronged with people when three men were seen pushing their way to the front.
>
> They hailed a boat and were being rowed frantically to the departing steamer when another man appeared, waving his arms excitedly.
>
> Getting no response from the rowing boat, he dived into the water and swam furiously towards the steamer. His progress was watched with tense interest by the holidaymakers aboard.
>
> Capt. Couves, seeing the man's plight, stopped the vessel just as a fifth man put in his appearance and waved to the people in the boat.
>
> The rowing boat returned and picked up the man from the water and the other man from the shore. The five late comers then boarded the Devonia.
>
> "'It was just like a kinema show,'" said an official of P. & A. Campbell Ltd. "'The passengers thoroughly enjoyed the man's plucky efforts to reach the vessel and cheered him heartily. He was little the worse for his experience and, when hauled aboard, seemed to think he had had an excellent joke. After wringing out his wet clothes he drank to the health of his fellow passengers in Benedictine, a bottle of which he held up triumphantly in his hand. In spite of the delay we reached Brighton at our scheduled time.'"

The 1924 season began on Wednesday 16th. April with the **GLEN AVON** on the Cardiff to Weston ferry. On the same day the **RAVENSWOOD** left Bristol for Newhaven, with two passengers, to begin the South Coast sailings.

The Easter weekend was marred by a tragedy in which the **GLEN USK** was implicated, although it was later proved that she was in no way to blame.

The River Usk, on its course downstream, carried with it quantities of small coal, emanating from the mines which lined its valley. The tidal flow caused the coal to be deposited on the mud flats where the river entered the Severn estuary at Newport.

Certain residents of the town, in order to supplement their meagre incomes, journeyed in open boats to the "patch", as it was known, at the river mouth, to collect the coal which they then sold to the local power station. It was a lucrative but dangerous business. Their boats, often ships lifeboats which had been purchased cheaply from Cashmore's, the ship breakers yard on the bank of the river, were unpowered and relied on the ebb and flow of the tides to take their occupants to and from the patch. They were usually manned by a few people, with an oar for steering, and were frequently loaded with so much coal, making them so low in the water, that less than a foot of freeboard was visible.

On the morning of Easter Monday 21st. April 1924, one such boat, the 30ft. **RUBY,** was taken by four occupants to the patch where they spent most of the day loading her with coal. The **GLEN USK,** on her way to Newport for an evening cruise to Bristol, passed up river shortly before they floated off the patch at 18.30.

One of the occupants, Thomas Henson, later described the course of events. He stated that from the patch to the Transporter bridge was a distance of about two miles. They went up the right hand side of the fairway but took a middle course when about fifty yards from the bridge in order to see if anything was coming around the bend. They knew that the **GLEN USK** would be returning but they did not expect her so soon. When they first saw the steamer the **RUBY** was about fifty yards from the east bank.The **GLEN USK** was about 100 yards off and they started pulling for the east bank.

On the **GLEN USK,** Capt. William Riddell saw the **RUBY,** blew a warning blast on the whistle and stopped the engines. The flood tide forced her almost broadside on across the river and the **RUBY** reached a position parallel to her at a distance of about 70 yards from her port side. At the same time the **RUBY** became swamped with water and quickly sank. Three of her occupants jumped into the river and were drowned. Thomas Henson survived by clinging to the oar and was picked up by the crew of the **GLEN USK,** who had hastily launched the stern lifeboat.

Initial reports intimated that it was the **GLEN USK'S** wash which had swamped the **RUBY,** but at the subsequent inquest several witnesses testified that by the time the two vessels were parallel there was no wash whatsoever from the **GLEN USK.** It was the considered opinion of those witnesses, all of them experienced boatmen, that the **RUBY** was too far out into the fairway and that she was dangerously overloaded with about 8 tons of coal. They had seen her caught in an eddy which swung her around as though she were on a pivot, and it was the eddy that had swamped her. The Coroner returned a verdict of "Accidental drowning" on the three men.

Since her acquisition by Campbell's the **LADY MOYRA** appeared to be dogged by bad luck. In addition to her accident at the end of the previous season, on Monday 23rd. May, while lying at the Mardyke Wharf, Bristol, ready to start her season, she was struck by the steamship **VIRAGO.** The **LADY MOYRA** sustained damage to her bow which necessitated a further spell in dry dock before she was able to enter service.

An innovation of the 1924 season was Sunday sailings in the Bristol Channel. Although the White Funnel steamers had run regularly on Sundays on the South Coast, in the Bristol Channel it just wasn't done! The first, somewhat tentative, Sunday passenger carrying sailing was an afternoon cruise along the Gower Coast from Swansea, by the **GLEN GOWER** on 29th. June.

It was not until later in the season that the company ventured to make Sunday calls at Ilfracombe. The residents were most unhappy about this development and some very indignant letters appeared in the local press suggesting, among other things, that the Welsh passengers would visit the town simply to frequent the local public houses because their own country's hostelries were closed on the Sabbath.

The story is told of a reporter who regularly visited Ilfracombe pier on Sunday evenings, notebook at the ready, eager to report any incidents of drunken or unseemly behaviour. It appears that he was singularly unlucky in his quest; the passengers displayed exemplary sobriety and respectability, giving no cause whatsoever for complaint.

Gradually the Sunday sailings to Ilfracombe became accepted and it became the custom for the residents and holidaymakers alike to visit the pier and St. James's Park, overlooking the harbour, on Sunday evenings to watch the departure of the steamers bound for South Wales and to listen to the Hymns, sung with great fervour and expertise, by the impromptu "choirs" formed by the Welsh passengers.

The summer was, again, one of appalling weather; the third in succession. The South Coast services were particularly badly affected, the three steamers spending day after day stormbound in Newhaven harbour. Fortunately the weather was kind for the duration of the Naval Review, held in Spithead at the end of July, and the steamers earned good revenue with their trips to view the assembled fleet of warships. The South Coast sailings were once again taken by the **DEVONIA, RAVENSWOOD** and **BRIGHTON BELLE.** The latter, incidentally, having had her large after saloon windows replaced by portholes, and Marconi Wireless installed with its attendant jigger.

Towards the end of the season an unfortunate calamity had a most frustrating effect on the Bristol sailings. On the morning of Saturday 6th. September the **BRITANNIA** had embarked over 400 passengers at Hotwells Landing Stage when a message was received informing Capt. Taylor that the 965 ton, William Sloane cargo steamer, **ETTRICK,** had capsized and sunk in Sea Mills Reach, River Avon, a little way upstream from the Horseshoe Bend. She blocked the river and all of the subsequent White Funnel Fleet sailings to and from Bristol were cancelled for several weeks, while repeated attempts to salvage the **ETTRICK** failed. The **BRITANNIA** remained "locked in" at Bristol and finished her season early, on Thursday 11th. September. The Bristol sailings were rescheduled to start and finish at Avonmouth, passengers being conveyed to and from the docks by train.

By the end of September, although the **ETTRICK** was still ashore, the river was cleared sufficiently for the steamers to pass, but the revised schedule of sailings in the meantime, with its inevitable restrictions, led to a loss of revenue which compounded the already poor trading brought about by the bad weather.

The **LADY MOYRA** had finished her season and was laid up for the winter in the Royal Edward Dock, Avonmouth, on Friday 19th. September, but was able to make her way up to the Floating Harbour, Bristol, on Thursday 2nd. October.

It was not until the end of November that the **ETTRICK** was towed up river from Sea Mills Reach. She was eventually broken up at Portishead in 1925.

The poor weather continued right up to the end of the season, when the **GLEN AVON** made the last ferry crossings on Saturday 11th. October.

Problems had been encountered by the returning South Coast steamers. The **DEVONIA'S** passage from Brighton to Bristol passed uneventfully but the **RAVENSWOOD** had to take shelter, for six hours, in Torbay and the **BRIGHTON BELLE** was delayed for a day in Falmouth.

The memorandum book for 1923 contains a number of references to the paddle steamer, **QUEEN OF THE SOUTH,** the only other vessel on the Sussex coast that season She ran mainly from Eastbourne, in direct competition with the **RAVENSWOOD,** and the references in the memorandum book are a comparison of the timings of the two vessels. The Campbell competition, however, proved to be too much and she was offered for sale at the end of the 1923 season. During the course of 1924 it was reported to the board that Capt. Alec had inspected her and considered it advisable to purchase her at about £2,500. However, the poor trading figures for the season precluded any further thoughts on the matter. She was eventually sold to the New Medway Steam Packet Co. and left the South Coast.

Aboard the CAMBRIA approaching Lynmouth Foreland in the early 1920's. (ERK)

The WESTWARD HO at the A. & J. Inglis yard, Pointhouse, Glasgow, during re-boilering. June/July 1921. (CCC)

The WESTWARD HO, with her sails set, fogbound at Avonmouth on the morning of Saturday 1st. October 1921, the day after her collision with the schooner, MARGARET WEST. She had left Cardiff at 05.00 and entered the Avon an hour later, but owing to thick fog she turned at Pill and spent the rest of the day at Avonmouth, making her way to Bristol that evening. The damage to her port paddle-box can be seen. (CCC)

The earliest known view of the new White Funnel steamer – No. 377 – at the Ailsa Shipbuilding Co's yard at Troon. Tuesday 23rd. August 1921. (CCC)

The launch of No. 377, Tuesday 14th. February, 1922. The gentleman in the light raincoat, fifth from the right of the photograph, is Capt. Alec. Next but one on his right is his wife, Ethel, holding the be-ribboned bottle of champagne with which she named the ship, GLEN GOWER. (CCC)

45

The GLEN GOWER slides into the waters of the Firth of Clyde. (CCC)

The GLEN GOWER fitting out. May 1922. (CCC)

The GLEN GOWER nearing completion of her trials, Wednesday 24th. May 1922. Her funnels are scorched from intense heat generated by pushing her to her limit. Her mean trial speed of 17.25 knots was 0.25 faster than the guaranteed speed. The ALBION's engines, although nearly 30 years old, proved to be as good as new. (CCC)

The GLEN GOWER leaves the Cumberland Basin to berth at Hotwells Landing Stage in readiness for her maiden trip, to Ilfracombe. Friday 2nd. June 1922. (ERK)

One of the occasional visits to Watchet. The RAVENSWOOD arrives in August 1922. (CCC)

A Saturday evening at Ilfracombe. The GLEN GOWER, WESTWARD HO, DEVONIA and RAVENSWOOD await their return trips. August 1922. (CCC)

The GLEN GOWER leaving Swansea. 1923/1924. (CCC)

Capt. Duncan Smith and Chief Officer Frederick Nunn on the bridge of the GLEN GOWER at Mumbles Pier, in the early 1920's. (CCC)

The CAMBRIA dips her bow into the oncoming swell as she sails westward from Ilfracombe in 1922. (CCC)

The LADY MOYRA arriving at Ilfracombe Pier in the 1920's (HGO)

A cartoon from a 1920's Swansea newspaper. "Disembarking passenger to embarking passenger: 'Nice trip, glorious boat, but what a rotten road!'" The exposed Swansea to Ilfracombe sailings were a frequent cause of "mal de mer'. Inset: The Bristol Channel and District Guide's suggested remedy.

An early post-war view of the DEVONIA turning at Boulogne. Possibly after her first crossing on Tuesday 22nd. May 1923. (CCC)

The BRIGHTON BELLE on the south coast in 1923. (CCC)

Aboard the BRIGHTON BELLE in the early 1920's. (CCC)

The QUEEN OF THE SOUTH, the steamer in which the Campbells expressed an interest, leaving Brighton in 1923. (CCC)

Naval Review sailings of the DEVONIA and BRIGHTON BELLE, 1924.

GLEN GOWER & BRITANNIA at Ilfracombe in the 1920's (HGO)

CAMBRIA arriving at Bristol. June 1924. (ERK)

GLEN USK at the Mardyke Wharf, Bristol, in the 1920's. (HGO)

Chapter 3 – 1925/1927

The weather during the summer of 1925, while showing an improvement over the past few years, was nevertheless somewhat indifferent, but the season progressed reasonably well with little incident.

The **GLEN AVON**, however, ran into difficulties on Friday 15th. May when on an afternoon trip from Weston to Minehead. At about 16.30 a heavy sea fog rolled in from the west. She sailed from Minehead at 19.38 in a fresh westerly wind, and proceeded at slow speed, with all of her crew on the lookout. At about 21.00 speed was further reduced as the fog became more and more dense. Soundings were being taken and indicated plenty of water just prior to the steamer grounding on the submerged Howe Rock, off Brean Down, at 21.12. Her lifeboats were swung out, lifebelts were issued to all passengers and distress rockets were fired. The bilges were examined throughout the vessel but showed no signs of taking on water. Capt. Henry Chidgey kept her engines at "slow astern", the tide being about 1½ hours to the flood and flowing very quickly. (The memorandum book records that this particular tide rose 3ft. 6ins. above its predicted level at Bristol).

She floated off the rock at 21.47 and proceeded slowly to Weston where she arrived at 22.12, still shrouded in thick fog. She eventually arrived at Cardiff, in clearing weather, at 23.35 without further mishap. After ten days in Stothert's Dry Dock, Bristol, she re-entered service on Friday 29th. May.

A certain amount of argument still continued concerning Sunday sailings. One of the last bastions of Sunday sailing objectors was Clevedon; to quote one of the town's councillors:-

> "The question of permitting pleasure steamers to call at the pier was raised at the Clevedon Council meeting; subsequently a deputation was arranged to interview a committee of the Council at which it was my duty to preside. The deputation consisted of several business men, and their only submission was that by allowing the steamers to call on Sundays it would be a relief to the local rates. To each of the deputation I asked the same question: would they be prepared to continue their business on the Sabbath Day for profit? Their reply was in the negative. How then, I wanted to know, were we as a Council justified in taking the responsibility of desecrating the Sabbath for the sake of obtaining revenue from the rates?

Ultimately, however, the Council decided to allow the steamers to call on Sundays, at first by way of a number of evening cruises in mid-July 1925 and then, gradually, at any time. To quote the Clevedon councillor again:-

> "... and so the thin end of the wedge was driven in, and now life in Clevedon does not compare with those days of old. What have we profited in body, soul and spirit; and what is the gain, if any, financially?"

By coincidence, on the afternoon of Sunday 5th. July 1925, the **GLEN GOWER** was running a cruise from Port Talbot. On backing out her starboard cant line carried away and fouled the rudder head, causing it to twist. The Port Talbot pilot cutter took her in tow to Swansea where the tug **FOXHOUND** towed her up the river to Pockett's Wharf. The Port Talbot passengers were taken home by train and the evening cruise from Swansea, for which about 800 passengers were waiting, had to be cancelled. The **GLEN GOWER** was towed to Bristol, for repairs, on the following day and was out of service for a week. All sailings from Swansea were taken by the **CAMBRIA** in the meantime. Those possessed of a more fervent religious nature were only too eager to point out that this incident was just retribution on the company for running on Sundays.

The season continued with the trips following their usual routine. This would be an appropriate point to look more closely at the pattern of those sailings and to analyse some of the activities of the steamers on a typical weekday and Saturday.

The memorandum book states that on Monday 22nd June 1925 high water at Bristol was at 07.59 and the weather was fine with a fresh, westerly wind.

The **BRITANNIA** was the main Bristol steamer and had the arduous duty of running the long, Bristol-down channel services to Ilfracombe and beyond. This particular day, however, found her at Cardiff, leaving at 07.15 for a day trip to Bristol. She then sailed at 09.40 on a day trip from Bristol to Clevedon and Cardiff, arriving at about mid-day. She remained at the Pier Head until 17.15, when she returned to Clevedon and Bristol, finally running a cruise from Bristol at 19.30 to Chepstow, arriving back in Bristol at 21.45, ready to resume her down channel sailings on the following day.

Before the start of the season the **BARRY** had been renamed, taking the name of the first Bristol Channel White Funnel steamer, **WAVERLEY.** She was usually based at Cardiff but sailed light from Barry on the morning of the 22nd. June to replace the **BRITANNIA** for the day. She then left Bristol at 08.45 for Clevedon, Weston, Lynmouth and Ilfracombe with a cruise to Bideford Bay returning from Ilfracombe to Bristol at 16.20. After her arrival at Bristol she left for Clevedon and Cardiff at 21.00, thus returning her to her normal station. This sailing also gave those passengers who had sailed from Cardiff on the **BRITANNIA** that morning the option of a long day in Bristol with a later return to Cardiff.

The **GLEN USK**, based at Newport, left at 09.30 for Weston, where a number of her 520 passengers took the opportunity to change on to the **WAVERLEY**, coming down from Bristol on her way to Ilfracombe. The **GLEN USK** then anchored off Weston over the low water period until returning from Birnbeck Pier, at 16.40, to Newport. A further crossing to Weston at 18.10 again connected with the **WAVERLEY,** en route from Ilfracombe to Bristol. She returned again from Weston, at 19.40, arriving back at Newport in time to run a cruise, at 21.15, to the Bell Buoy, off the mouth of the River Usk, with 101 passengers, before ending her day at Newport at about 23.00.

The **WESTWARD HO,** which frequently supplemented the Bristol and Cardiff - down channel sailings, followed a slightly different pattern that day. She sailed light from Bristol, at about 07.30, to take 668 passengers on a day trip from Sharpness, at 09.00, to Weston and Ilfracombe. The sailings from Sharpness were run in conjunction with the railways and connecting trains brought passengers from the Forest of Dean, Birmingham, Swindon, Cheltenham and Gloucester and were waiting to take them to their destinations on their return.

The **CAMBRIA** took the 09.35 day trip from her usual base, Cardiff, to Barry, Minehead, Lynmouth, Ilfracombe and Clovelly.

The **GLEN AVON,** the usual ferry steamer, made five round trips from Cardiff to Weston, beginning at 07.45 and finishing at 22.00, having carried 3411 passengers during the day.

The **GLEN GOWER** left Swansea at 09.00 for Ilfracombe and Lundy Island, arriving back in Swansea at 20.45, having called off Clovelly in both directions.

The **LADY MOYRA** was not yet in service. Because of her high fuel consumption she was usually late to start and early to finish. She had been moored at St. Augustine's Bridge, City Centre, Bristol, for the King's visit on Tuesday 9th. June, when over 500 spectators boarded her. On Monday 22nd. June she left Stothert's Dry Dock in readiness to begin her season.

The main stations of the steamers were Bristol, Newport, Cardiff and Swansea. Ilfracombe was not a base in its own right, in that the ships infrequently berthed there overnight. Nevertheless, the town was given an excellent service. On Monday 22nd. June, for example, the residents and visitors were given the choice of a cruise to Bideford Bay, two landing trips to Clovelly or a landing trip to Lundy.

The three South Coast steamers were, like the Bristol Channel fleet, employed on their routine duties. The **DEVONIA** left Palace Pier, Brighton, at 10.45 and the West Pier at 11.00 for Worthing and Cowes with 335 passengers, returning direct to Brighton at 16.30, with a train connection for Worthing.

The **BRIGHTON BELLE** made three cruises from Brighton "To view shipping" in the channel, carrying a total of 671 passengers.

The **RAVENSWOOD** sailed between Hastings and Eastbourne, making two round trips, incorporating two cruises in the channel, one from Hastings and one from Eastbourne, carrying a total of 557 passengers.

Saturday sailings were somewhat different as they gained much smaller revenue from the day trippers. This was the day on which passengers travelled to and from their holiday destinations, and the company organised its sailings to accommodate them. To illustrate this, the memorandum book entries for Saturday 1st. August 1925 will serve as a typical example.

The **BRITANNIA,** having lain at Ilfracombe over the previous night, left at 09.30 for Lynmouth, Cardiff, Clevedon and Bristol. This meant that North Devon residents had the opportunity of time ashore at those destinations and that returning holidaymakers could make an early start for home. Her return trip from Bristol arrived at Ilfracombe at about 20.00, she then left at 22.30 with 149 passengers and arrived at Bristol at 03.18 on the morning of Sunday 2nd. August.

The **WESTWARD HO,** from Barry, and the **LADY MOYRA,** from Cardiff and Minehead, also ran day trips to Ilfracombe. On her return to Cardiff the **WESTWARD HO** supplemented the ferry sailings, making two round trips with a total of 1086 passengers.

The **GLEN USK** ran two trips from Newport to Weston and the **WAVERLEY** ran the ever popular afternoon cruise from Cardiff to Clevedon and Bristol. Both ships also helped out on the ferry, on which a total of no less than 8335 passengers were carried during the day.

The **CAMBRIA** made two round trips to Ilfracombe, one from Bristol and Cardiff at 05.30, returning to Cardiff at 10.30 and another from Cardiff at 14.30 which returned to Barry, arriving at 20.00.

The **GLEN GOWER** started her day at 07.45 and made three round trips between Ilfracombe, Mumbles and Swansea, finally berthing for the night in the early hours of the following morning. Cruises out of Ilfracombe on Saturdays were the exception rather than the rule as there was little demand. The steamers would normally lay at the pier awaiting their return sailings.

On the South Coast things were also a little different; Saturdays were quiet days. It was usual for the **DEVONIA** to make an afternoon sailing to the Isle of Wight, which she did on 1st. August, taking 308 passengers from Brighton to Ventnor. The **BRIGHTON BELLE** ran a morning and evening cruise in the channel with a total of 698 passengers, and the **RAVENSWOOD** was off service; not unusual for the South Coast steamers.

This onslaught of facts and figures serves to illustrate the planning behind the timetables. When one considers that all this organisation had to fit in with the tides, one can appreciate the enormity of the task.

The rise and fall of the Bristol Channel tides, the second largest in the world, had a major influence over the pattern of sailings. High water was fifty minutes later each day and the tidal cycle lasted fourteen days.

To take Bristol as an example; the optimum departure time for day trips was about 09.00, but the steamers could leave at any time between 06.00 and lunchtime, depending on the time of high water, the departure time of the return trip being adjusted correspondingly. On the days when the tides precluded day trips, either shorter, local cruises took place or, exceptionally, the steamer would be off service.

Similar situations prevailed at most of the up channel ports, one exception being Barry, where the pontoon was accessible at any state of the tide. Consequently, trips to, and cruises from Barry were scheduled for the low water period. On other "low water" cruises the steamer would leave her point of departure on the last of the tide and make her way down channel to the Monkstone Beacon off Penarth, the Breaksea Light Vessel off Barry, or around the Holms, thus keeping her in sufficiently deep water before her return on the first of the flood.

Swansea was available at most states of the tide, apart from low water springs, but it was often necessary for the steamers to berth at the South Dock jetty when their usual berth at Pockett's Wharf, further upstream, was not accessible. The steamer frequently had to be moved, sometimes in the middle of the night, (most unpopular with the crew), to position her for her next departure.

By way of a further complication the largest rise and fall occurred on the spring tides so, whereas certain landing places were unavailable on such tides, on the neap tides, with their smaller rise and fall,landing was possible.

Yet another consideration was the positioning of each steamer in readiness for her next sailing, ensuring that unprofitable, light running was kept to a minimum.

All these factors combined to make the scheduling of trips appear to be an organisational nightmare, but the network of sailings did not come about overnight.

They evolved over many years of experience, trial and error. If all this appears complicated, spare a thought for the ship's pursers, who had to battle with the intricacies of ticket sales on a very complex variety of services.

In spite of the company's meticulous planning, the weather always had the last word and gave rise to that well known phrase printed on all the timetables, "Weather and circumstances permitting". The memorandum book entry for Monday 27th. July is reproduced on page 72. All of that day's sailings were either curtailed or cancelled!

The **RAVENSWOOD'S** trip to Boulogne on Sunday 23rd. August deserves particular mention. She left Hastings at 11.00 with 435 passengers on what is believed to be the last sailing to France by an open foredeck paddle steamer. The Board of Trade decreed that such ships should no longer cross the channel. As a consequence the **RAVENSWOOD** was withdrawn from South Coast service and was replaced, from the following season, by the **WAVERLEY.**

Under the command of Capt. Frank Weeks the **WAVERLEY** left Bristol, light, at 06.20 on Monday 29th. March 1926 and arrived at Newhaven at 10.09 on the following morning. She opened the season on Thursday 1st. April and made her first crossing to Boulogne on Easter Sunday 4th. April.

The Bristol Channel season began with a mishap. On the evening of Good Friday 2nd. April the **GLEN USK** was taking an evening cruise from Cardiff to Bristol. In the River Avon, at 20.10, she encountered the steamer **SEAFORTH,** outward bound, which forced her against the rocks on the west bank of the river, causing damage to her starboard paddle. She made Bristol at slow speed and entered the Floating Harbour for repairs. The return trip to Cardiff was taken by the **BRITANNIA,** after completing her day trip to Ilfracombe.

Shortly after Easter, Penarth Pier was once again open to the steamers. During the early part of the Great War it had been requisitioned by the Royal Engineers, and by the end of the hostilities, although the main body of the pier was sound, the landing stage was in need of a considerable amount of repair, owing to the lack of maintenance. Campbell's expressed an interest in its purchase but an estimated £10,000 for the necessary repairs put it out of their reach. Its owners, the Penarth Pier Co., were in financial difficulties and it was eventually sold to the Penarth Urban District Council on 1st. August 1924, for the sum of £5000. After further delays the repairs commenced in May 1925, when the wooden piles were replaced by ferro-concrete, quite an innovation for the time. The renovations were completed in February 1926 and the official re-opening took place on Wednesday 7th. April, when the **GLEN AVON** made the first call, to take the Civic dignitaries on a trip to Weston.

1926 was to prove a most difficult season. Industrial unrest increased and on Saturday 1st. May the miners began a strike which was to last until mid-November. At midnight on Monday 3rd. May a general strike commenced, called by the TUC in support of the miners. Within twenty-four hours the wheels of industry had ground to a halt. There were no trains, no trams or buses and no newspapers; steelworks closed and the docks lay idle. However, more than 300,000 volunteers rallied to the Government's cause when people from all walks of life temporarily took on the jobs of the strikers.

Coal supplies became limited and very erratic and led to a late start for most of the steamers. The **WAVERLEY** was out of service because of the shortage of coal and lay at anchor off Brighton from Monday 3rd. to Thursday 6th. May, when she proceeded to the Palace Pier. Her crew had been given 48 hours notice and the Bristol contingent disembarked to be taken home by charabanc. The **WAVERLEY** then made her way to Newhaven harbour to lay up.

The General Strike was called off, as ineffectual, on Thursday 13th. May. The **WAVERLEY** eventually obtained enough coal at Newhaven to resume sailing and managed to reach Boulogne on Wednesday 26th. May, where she took on a good supply of coal.

It should be pointed out that the South Coast steamers which crossed to France coaled at Boulogne, whenever possible, the best quality Scottish coal, which the company favoured, being cheaper in France than in the UK. The operation was carried out after the passengers had disembarked when a barge, with its crane, would be brought alongside the steamer and the coal would be lifted into the chutes leading down from the deck into the bunkers. It was a particularly dirty operation necessitating a good washing down before the passengers re-embarked for the return journey.

The **WAVERLEY** lost intermittent days sailings because of the coal shortage but fared better than the Bristol Channel fleet, where only the **GLEN AVON** and the **GLEN USK** were in service. The **BRITANNIA** came out on Sunday 23rd. May but a note in the memorandum book states, "no coal released". A week later she, and the **GLEN USK** were again laid up in Bristol, leaving the **GLEN AVON** alone on the ferry.

The **GLEN USK** came out again on Saturday 5th. June and on the following Monday ran a non-landing cruise from Bristol up the River Wye to Chepstow. She then ran to Ilfracombe on Thursday 10th. June, the first down channel trip that year.

The **DEVONIA** and her sister ship, **LADY MOYRA,** were particularly heavy on fuel, and in view of the situation in the Bristol Channel, ironically on the doorstep of the massive South Wales coalfield, the **LADY MOYRA** was laid up in Bristol throughout the season. It was anticipated, however, that the **DEVONIA**, like the **WAVERLEY,** would be able to coal at Boulogne, and on the strength of this she was brought into service. She left Bristol, Cardiff and Ilfracombe on Tuesday 29th. June and discharged her 69 passengers at Brighton on the following day after an uneventful round trip. Soon after beginning her season a crack was discovered in the bottom of her boiler necessitating her withdrawal, for repairs, for three days. She re-entered service on Sunday 11th. July with a day trip to Boulogne.

The weather that summer was the best since 1921. The late start of the steamers, because of the coal strike, was therefore as frustrating as it was unfortunate. There were long spells of warm and sunny weather but they were interspersed with heavy and sultry days, which led to that worst of conditions - dense sea fog.

The **DEVONIA** was fogbound in the English Channel on the night of Sunday 11th. July, with 200 passengers aboard, and was not able to make port until the Monday morning. The newspapers reported:-

> "The Devonia left Boulogne at 18.00 and, a few miles out, ran into dense banks of fog. Capt. Couves had to go dead slow, but when he neared Eastbourne the fog lifted and the Eastbourne and Hastings passengers were landed. The

Devonia then started on the final stage of her trip, but when she was rounding Beachy Head the fog became thicker than ever. The voyage continued at a snail's pace, the only sounds heard by the passengers being the whistles of unseen ships passing up and down the channel. At daybreak she anchored off the Palace Pier, Brighton, and groped her way to the landing stage to discharge her passengers at about 05.00 on Monday 12th. July".

On that same morning, much of the Bristol Channel was shrouded in particularly thick banks of fog. The **CAMBRIA** left Cardiff at 08.20, in fine weather, for Weston, Minehead, Lynmouth, Ilfracombe and Clovelly. After leaving Lynmouth she ran into one of the dense fog patches, she was slowed down and lookouts were posted all around the ship but, at 12.40 she ran on to the rocks at Rillage Point, a few miles east of Ilfracombe. The "Western Mail" continues:-

"The officer who was on the foredeck asked the passengers to move to the stern. Capt. Livingstone, who was on the bridge, quickly allayed the fears of all on board.

Naturally such an untoward happening caused some alarm, but the calmness of the master, his officers and the ship's company had the effect greatly desired and there was not a single moment of panic. The crew at once took stations at the ship's boats and everything was immediately in readiness for lowering them.

Fog signals were fired and these caused some alarm on shore and on Ilfracombe pier, where people stood peering through the fog. From the harbour, motor boats, some with punts trailing behind, raced to the rescue. By the time these reached the **CAMBRIA** her own boats had been lowered and the 146 passengers, most of them relishing the novel situation, had been rowed to the rocks and beach close by.

Many of the passengers attempted the hazardous task of climbing the cliffs bordering the main road to the Devon watering place and were successful, but the majority waited until everyone had been safely landed before the boats took them to Ilfracombe harbour. Several journeys had to be made. The Ilfracombe lifeboat, which had been launched under somewhat difficult conditions through the shallow depth of the water, arrived on the scene. She was followed by a fleet of small craft and, together, they assisted in landing the passengers".

The **CAMBRIA** re-floated and proceeded, at 16.30, under her own steam to Ilfracombe, where she remained overnight for temporary repairs to be made, although there was little damage. The **GLEN USK,** also on a trip from Cardiff to Ilfracombe, had stood by during her grounding and took the **CAMBRIA'S** passengers home.

The **CAMBRIA** left Ilfracombe at 13.40 on the following day, again under her own steam, and sailed direct to Bristol where she entered Hill's Dry Dock for a survey and permanent repairs.

Following the incident, the passengers were unstinting in their praise of the way in which Capt. Livingstone had handled the situation. It therefore comes as something of a surprise to find the following, rather terse, paragraph in the minutes of a board meeting which took place later in July:-

"Capt. Alec referred to the mishap of the Cambria on 12th. July 1926 and it was decided to retire Capt. A. Livingstone: to allow him £3 per week, at the discretion of the directors and to write a suitable letter, thanking him for his long and faithful service".

It was an unfortunate end to a most distinguished career of over thirty years. He was associated for most of that time with the **CAMBRIA**, the ship which he knew and handled so well. It was Capt. Livingstone who took the **CAMBRIA** safely around Land's End through the ferocious gale at the end of August 1908: probably the worst storm ever encountered by a White Funnel steamer.

It must be acknowledged that throughout its history the company maintained a remarkably accident free safety record: a record which owed much to the calibre of its officers. Its main sphere of operations, the Bristol Channel, was a most treacherous area and, whereas the mariners of today have a vast array of sophisticated navigational equipment at their disposal, the Campbell masters, exposed to all weathers on their open bridges, had only a compass! Their "navigational aids" were their seamanship, experience and good eyesight.

The **CAMBRIA** re-entered service on Thursday 22nd. July, under the command of Capt. Jack George, and was based at Swansea for the rest of the season, replacing the **GLEN GOWER** which had been moved up channel to run from Cardiff. Capt. William Riddell took command of the **CAMBRIA** at the end of July, with Capt. George transferring to the **GLEN USK,** the steamer with which he was associated for some years.

Jack George was destined to become the commodore of the White Funnel Fleet. He was a quiet, rather shy man who, like Capt. Livingstone, was small in stature but a giant in terms of seamanship. He had joined the company at the age of 14 as a chocolate boy, selling confectionary aboard the **WESTWARD HO.** He became a steward, deckhand and ordinary seaman before going "deep-sea" and commencing training as an officer. He later returned to his home in Congresbury, near Bristol, and re-joined the Campbell fleet.

The fine weather of 1926 continued. The **DEVONIA** had enjoyed a successful season on the South Coast and had experienced no problems with coaling in Boulogne. However, in view of her high fuel consumption it was considered prudent to replace her, at the end of the busiest part of the season, with a less "hungry" steamer. Her substitute was the **GLEN GOWER,** which left Cardiff at 12.00 on Thursday 31st. August for Penarth, Ilfracombe and the South Coast. She carried 177 passengers on the trip and arrived, for the first time, at Brighton, 23 hours, 27 minutes out of Ilfracombe, at 16.25 on Wednesday 1st. September. Capt. Oswald Morris commanded her on the round trip but she was then taken over by Capt. Couves and made her first crossing to Boulogne on Friday 3rd. September.

On the same day Capt. Morris took over the **DEVONIA** to bring her home, leaving the West Pier, Brighton, at 09.32 and arriving at Ilfracombe at 07.43 on Saturday 4th. September. She then took the 14.00 single trip to Penarth, Clevedon and Bristol, entering the Floating Harbour that evening to lay up for the winter.

The miners' strike lasted for six months and the effects of the coal shortages had been felt only too keenly by the White Funnel Fleet. Although the fine weather generated high passenger figures, the overall loss of sailings, especially because of the late start, meant a poor financial result. Several economy measures had already been taken; the number of staff at the Weston and Ilfracombe offices were reduced earlier in the year and the ketch, **LARK,** purchased by the company in 1920 to carry coal to the steamers in Bristol, was sold. At the October board meeting, Alec was instructed to look into a reduction of winter wages.

At the end of the season, and during the months of the following winter, the **GLEN GOWER** featured, time and again, in the headlines of the national press, when she was involved, albeit rather tenuously, in a series of events culminating in a mystery which remains unsolved. The story is intriguing.

On Wednesday 6th. October 1926 the **GLEN GOWER,** on the last trip of her season, sailed from Brighton, Eastbourne and Hastings, to Boulogne, where she disembarked 316 passengers. Two of those passengers were 24 year-old May Daniels and her companion, Marcella McCarthy. Both ladies were nurses, on leave from the Chiswick and Ealing Isolation Hospital in London. They spent their time ashore exploring Boulogne until shortly before the **GLEN GOWER** was due to sail on the return trip. Nurse Daniels entered a public lavatory, while her friend waited outside, but did not re-appear! After a fruitless search, Nurse McCarthy returned to the quay in time to see the **GLEN GOWER** depart. Nurse Daniels had kept the return halves of their tickets and Nurse McCarthy was now stranded with insufficient money to return home. Curiously, the **GLEN GOWE**R returned with exactly the same number of passengers as she carried on the outward journey, despite the fact that the two ladies were not aboard. It should be mentioned that on the cross channel trips an accurate tally of passenger numbers was always kept.

Two days later, with the help of the British Consul, Nurse McCarthy was issued with a temporary passport, (un-necessary for day passengers), and returned to the UK, totally mystified by the disappearance of her friend and unable to throw any light whatsoever on the situation.

There were no further substantial developments until February 1927, when the body of Nurse Daniels was discovered in a field outside Boulogne. The corpse had been exposed to the ravages of the winter weather and the post-mortem was inconclusive. It showed, however, that her death had occurred several months before, and indicated that she may have been strangled. Near her body were a number of personal possessions including a hypodermic syringe and a quantity of morphine tablets, but there was no trace of the return halves of the steamer tickets. Nurse Daniels was buried in a Boulogne cemetery, and a charge of murder was brought against a person or persons unknown.

During the course of the investigation a number of theories were put forward, based on the available shreds of evidence. In the light of that evidence it appeared most likely that Nurse Daniels had visited Boulogne for the purpose of obtaining an abortion and that the whole trip was pre-arranged on her part. She fully intended taking Nurse McCarthy with her as a companion but kept her in complete ignorance of her true intentions. Many questions, however, remained un-answered: did Nurse Daniels plan on leaving her friend stranded? Did she expect that the operation would be carried out in time for them both to return on the **GLEN GOWER?** If so, what had happened to the return halves of the tickets? Had they simply been lost, or were they used by two people who returned to the UK in place of the nurses?

The discovery of the hypodermic syringe and the morphine tablets, relatively easily accessible to a nurse, as well as the fact that she wanted a colleague to accompany her, certainly add weight to the abortion theory. Whatever Nurse Daniels' intentions were, the procedure went horribly wrong, but whether she died as a direct result of an abortion, or whether she was murdered for some other reason will never be known. The "Nurse Daniels Mystery" remains unsolved!

To return to the Campbell history: with coal supplies back to normal the company experienced no problems in this respect during the 1927 season. The weather, on the other hand, was a different matter; wet and windy was, yet again, the order of the day and led to a serious disruption of sailings.

On the South Coast, the **DEVONIA** had a particularly nasty experience while returning from Boulogne on Friday 1st. July. She left at 18.30 and headed across the channel into a westerly wind which quickly increased to gale force. By 20.00 she was labouring, at slow speed, in very heavy seas, and arrived at Brighton at just after midnight, two hours late, having damaged herself considerably during the crossing. The memorandum book lists the following:-

> "Port forward wing door stove in; port forward lifeboat displaced; 1 porthole in ladies 2nd. class lavatory broken, also one in gents lavatory and two in stokehold; 1 square window, port side forward broken".

There were also a number of dented and buckled plates as well as broken furniture, smashed crockery and glasses, together with carpets and curtains soaked with sea water. She was off service in Newhaven, for repairs, on Saturday 2nd. July.

Although most of her 300 passengers found the trip a thoroughly unpleasant and frightening experience, they could hardly have been in better hands. Not only was the **DEVONIA** an excellent sea-boat, her master, Capt. William Couves, was an expert seaman. He was one of the company's most "colourful" characters, known to the South Coast passengers as "Bill", and was noted for his anecdotes and broad humour.

He was a Gravesend man, who went to sea at an early age and rose to the rank of captain when still quite young. At the turn of the century, aged about twenty, he commanded the large paddle tug, **CONQUEROR**, which carried passengers from Margate, Ramsgate, Deal and Dover, to France. Some years later he joined the "Belle" steamers and, after obtaining a Port of London Authority licence, was employed as a Thames pilot until his retirement in the late 1940's. He joined P. & A. Campbell Ltd. in 1923 and, having a Boulogne pilot's licence, went straight into the **DEVONIA**. Each winter, however, he returned to Gravesend and his piloting duties.

The immense pride which he took in the ships under his command can be illustrated by an incident which occurred one dark and overcast Saturday night, when returning to Brighton from the usual afternoon trip to the Isle of Wight. Approaching the West Pier, he was watching for the leading mark, oil lamp on the knuckle. The pier man had placed it a little further shorewards than it should have been, with the result that when he brought the ship in, fast as usual, the port sponson hit the knuckle pile with some force. Fortunately the damage was slight but Capt Couves kept the bosun and a carpenter up all night securing the belting iron which had come adrift, as he refused to take his ship to Boulogne on the following day, looking so disreputable.

In the Bristol Channel, bad weather was responsible for the cancellation of many sailings including a charter of the **CAMBRIA** and the **GLEN GOWER,** from Briton Ferry. The local newspapers reported the full details which are reproduced on Page 74.

On Saturday 2nd. July, however, a further charter from Briton Ferry was successfully run, and was obviously a very lucrative day. The **LADY MOYRA**, after missing the 1926 season, was back in service and left, in company with the **GLEN GOWER,** at 08.00, for Ilfracombe. The former carried 1161 passengers, and the latter, 843.

The gloomy season continued with little major incident, apart from a high percentage of curtailed or called-off trips, but drew to a close with a sting in its tail.

On the last trip of the season, on Monday 11th. October, the **GLEN AVON** left the Pier Head, Cardiff, at 17.30, with just under 200 passengers aboard. About twenty minutes after leaving Penarth, fog descended on the channel and she was compelled to drop anchor. At 22.00 conditions had not improved and Capt. Chidgey announced that the tide was too low to land at Weston for at least four hours so that, even if the fog lifted, the ship would have to remain where she was. One of the passengers stated:-

> "When the captain told us we would have to spend the night on board we looked around for entertainment. A whist drive was suggested but it was found that there was only one pack of cards aboard, and even that was incomplete. It was then decided to hold an impromptu concert in the saloon; some of the passengers made very good artistes and everyone joined in the spirit of making the best of a bad job.
>
> The captain and crew did everything possible to make the passengers comfortable. The few children aboard were looked after by a Cardiff doctor and were soon comfortably tucked up in improvised cots.
>
> After midnight those who wanted to sleep were given blankets and pillows. The settees and deck chairs were converted into beds for the more somnolent of the party, but they were few, and the jollifications among the elders went on until the small hours.
>
> We were provided with plenty of food and had a good supper and breakfast. There was only one misfortune, after a few hours there was not a cigarette on board!"

At 06.20 on the following morning the fog had cleared sufficiently for the **GLEN AVON** to proceed, and she berthed at Weston at 06.45.

Until early on Tuesday morning company officials were unable to supply any facts about the incident, only conjectures, although they had assumed that Capt. Chidgey had, on running into the fog, dropped anchor for safety. The vessel was one of the few of the company's ships not fitted with wireless and no messages could be sent to or from her.

The **GLEN AVON** eventually arrived at Cardiff at 10.00 on Tuesday 12th. October, twelve and a half hours overdue, and left that afternoon to lay up at Bristol.

CARRYING CAPACITY
OF THE "WHITE FUNNEL" STEAMERS.

P.S. "BRITANNIA".

On a No.	5	Certificate	(smooth water) about	... ...	1,700 passengers
,,	4	,,	(Weston, Cardiff, &c.)	...	1,023 ,,
,,	3	,,	(from Bristol to Lundy Island) ...		887 ,,
,,	2	,,	(United Kingdom) ...	... ...	458 ,,

P.S. "CAMBRIA."

On a No.	5	Certificate	(smooth water) about	... ...	1,500 passengers
,,	4	,,	(Weston, Cardiff, &c.)	...	969 ,,
,,	3	,,	(from Bristol to Lundy Island) ...		833 ,,
,,	2	,,	(United Kingdom) ...	... ...	420 ,,

P.S. "WESTWARD HO !"

On a No.	5	Certificate	(smooth water) about	... ...	1,500 passengers
,,	4	,,	(Weston, Cardiff, &c.)	...	968 ,,
,,	3	,,	(from Bristol to Lundy Island) ...		830 ,,
,,	2	,,	(United Kingdom) ...	... ...	437 ,,

P.S. "RAVENSWOOD."

On a No.	5	Certificate	(smooth water) about	... ...	1,200 passengers
,,	4	,,	(Weston, Cardiff, &c.)	...	819 ,,
,,	3	,,	(from Bristol to Lundy Island) ...		695 ,,
,,	2	,,		... ...	345 ,,

P.S. "GLEN AVON."

On a No.	5	Certificate	(smooth water)	... ...	1,550 passengers
,,	4	,,	(Weston, Cardiff, &c.)	...	1,066 ,,
,,	3	,,	(from Bristol to Lundy Island) ...		924 ,,
,,	2	,,	(United Kingdom) ...	... ...	508 ,,

P.S. "DEVONIA."

On a No.	4	Certificate	(Weston, Cardiff, &c.)	... ...	1,133 passengers
,,	3	,,	(from Bristol to Lundy Island) ...		1,015 ,,
,,	2	,,	(United Kingdom) ...	... ...	520 ,,

P.S. "GLEN USK."

On a No.	5	Certificate	(smooth water)	... about	1,700 passengers
,,	4	,,	(Weston, Cardiff, etc.)	,,	1,159 ,,
,,	3	,,	(from Bristol to Lundy Island)	,,	1,005 ,,
,,	2	,,	(United Kingdom) ...	...	523 ,,

P.S. "BARRY."

On a No.	4	Certificate	(Weston, Cardiff, &c.)	... ...	940 passengers
,,	3	,,	(from Bristol to Lundy Island) ...		816 ,,
,,	2	,,	(United Kingdom) ...	... ...	397 ,,

P.S. "GLEN GOWER."

On a No.	4	Certificate	(Weston, Cardiff, &c.)	... ...	1,242 passengers
,,	3	,,	(from Bristol to Lundy Island) ...		1,079 ,,
,,	2	,,	(United Kingdom) ...	... ...	552 ,,

P.S. "LADY MOYRA."

On a No.	4	Certificate	(Weston, Cardiff, etc.)	... ...	1,133 passengers
,,	3	,,	(From Bristol to Lundy Island) ...		1,015 ,,
,,	2	,,	(United Kingdom)	... ...	519 ,,

P.S. "BRIGHTON BELLE."

On a No.	4	Certificate	(Weston, Cardiff, etc.)	... ...	779 passengers
,,	3	,,	(from Bristol to Lundy Island) ...		714 ,,
,,	2	,,	(United Kingdom)	... ...	320 ,,

From the Bristol Channel & District Guide. 1924.   WESTWARD HO at Newport in the 1920's. (CCC)

The WESTWARD HO in dry dock at Bristol. Painting below the waterline has been completed and patches of rust have been treated with red lead before she returns to the water. (HGO)

The GLEN GOWER ready to be undocked from Stothert's Dry Dock. late 1920's. (HGO)

The GLEN GOWER ready for another season. (HGO)

To maintain their pristine condition painting and varnishing of the steamers continued throughout the season. The CAMBRIA, off service at Barry, has her funnel painted while the GLEN GOWER arrives alongside on her way down-channel. (CCC)

A seaman varnishes the foremast of the LADY MOYRA as she lies alongside Ilfracombe Pier with the WESTWARD HO. Monday 31st. August 1925. (CCC)

The RAVENSWOOD at Boulogne. Sunday 23rd. August, 1925. (CCC)

The DEVONIA coaling at Boulogne, 1920's. (HAA)

Capt. William Riddell berths the
LADY MOYRA at Milford Haven in
the 1920's. (ERK)

Capt. Edward Calvert on the bridge
of the GLEN USK. (ERK)

The CAMBRIA aground on Rillage Point. Wednesday 12th. July 1926. The GLEN USK stands by. (CCC)

The GLEN USK leaving Swansea in the 1920's. (HGO)

The CAMBRIA in the Avon. 1927. (CCC)

208 **JULY, 1925.** *31st Week.*

MONDAY 27 (208-157)
Gale of Wly wind, plenty of Sea. Heavy rain till late afternoon.

Britannia Locked out. Bristol to Clevedon, Cardiff, Minehead, Ilfracombe & Lynmouth & Ilfracombe at 10.0am : 194.
W. Taylor   didn't call.   didn't go beyond Cardiff.
  ✓   Return Cardiff 9.0pm Clevedon 9.50 and Bristol 10.33 p.m. & into Basin.
             didn't call.

Westward Ho Lying in Cumberland Basin 9.30am Trips to Clevedon, Weston Ilfracombe & Lundy : Cancelled.
J. Ashford.

Cambria Left Cardiff 9.35am but didn't proceed any further than Barry.
Livingstone

Lady Moyra Left Cardiff 7.45am for Ilfracombe & Newquay but returned.
G. Riddell

Waverley Left Cardiff 8.0am for Weston but had to return, remaining Trips Cancelled.
H. Mc Fadyen

Glen Avon All Ferry Trips Cancelled.
H. Chidgey

Glen Usk Left Newport for Weston at 9.30am but had to return.
O. V. Monies

Glen Gower Lying at Swansea Trip Cancelled.
Jas Smith

Devonia, Brighton Belle & Ravenswood. Trips Cancelled. SWly Gale & Rain .   "Weather permitting"
W. A. Evans   B. J. Hawkin   J. C. Peters.

72

The DEVONIA arriving at Hastings. 1927. (HGO)

The DEVONIA at Calais in the 1920's. (HAA)

SWEPT BY GREAT WAVES.

Big Neath Outing Abandoned.

PLEASURE BOAT'S BATTLE WITH SEA.

Hundreds of Neath residents were deprived of a day's holiday on Thursday, when, owing to the weather conditions, it was found impossible to fulfil the programme mapped out for the annual shop assistants' outing.

All the shops in the town had been closed for the day, and arrangements had been made for a trip to Ilfracombe by the s.s. Cambria, which was to pick up the passengers at Briton Ferry.

When the early arrivals reached Briton Ferry Docks at about 7.30 they found that the boat was not moored to the landing stage. About 8 o'clock she was able to get in, and the captain came ashore to telephone for instructions. The prospective passengers were not allowed to go aboard, and a member of the crew, in an interview, said, "It has taken us five and a half hours to come from Cardiff. The waves outside are like cliffs, and the decks were swept by them on our way in. We fellows are prepared to risk it, but we wouldn't dare take passengers. In any case, we wouldn't guarantee your landing at Ilfracombe."

About 9 o'clock the captain returned, and after consultation with those responsible for the arrangements, it was made known that the trip could not take place, and the disappointed, dejected and bedraggled crowd returned to their homes.

The Cambria later put out to sea with only the crew aboard.

THE TRIPPERS TRIPPED.

Weather Spoils the Shop Assistants' Outing.

Great disappointment was experienced at Neath and Briton Ferry this morning, when the annual outing of the Neath and district shop assistants had to be abandoned.

They had chartered the passenger steamer Glen Gower to make a trip to Ilfracombe, and she duly arrived at Briton Ferry, but the morning was so rough, foggy and wet that the owners deemed it imprudent to make the passage, and after a couple of hours of waiting the boat returned to Swansea, and the disappointed trippers returned to Neath by train.

The LADY MOYRA and GLEN GOWER at Briton Ferry.
Saturday 2nd. July 1927. (HGO)

74

Chapter 4 – 1928/1929

The **WAVERLEY** opened the 1928 South Coast sailings, and on Easter Sunday 8th. April made the first post-war crossing to Calais. The fine but cold Easter, although followed by snow during the following week, preceded a reasonably good summer.

On Wednesday 23rd. May the Prince of Wales visited Bristol; the **CAMBRIA,** at St. Augustines Bridge, City Centre, and the **LADY MOYRA,** in the Cumberland Basin were on display and dressed overall for the occasion.

The **RAVENSWOOD** was on the receiving end of an unfortunate incident, while lying at the landing stage at Newport, on Thursday 7th. June. A section of an old pontoon was being towed to Cashmore's yard when it broke loose. The flood tide carried it upstream and in passing the **RAVENSWOOD** struck her starboard paddle, causing the cancellation of her day's sailings while repairs were carried out. The **RAVENSWOOD**, from that season was commanded by Capt. Findlay Brander, a Scotsman, whose somewhat portly frame was to become a familiar sight on the Campbell steamers for many years.

The **GLEN GOWER,** commanded by Capt. Frederick Nunn, returning from Ilfracombe to Bristol on the evening of Friday 6th. July, collided with an outward bound steamer while rounding the Horseshoe Bend, River Avon. Her forward, port sponson was damaged and the repairs kept her out of service for a few days.

Apart from these minor mishaps the season progressed satisfactorily. Its most notable event was announced by the "South Wales Daily Post", under the headline, "A Rare Sight":-

> "What will be a rare sight to many people will be in evidence on Sunday 29th. July. A full-dressed American liner will pass up the channel on her way to Cardiff.
>
> This will be the **GEORGE WASHINGTON,** which is bringing to this country, from the USA and Canada, nearly 1000 passengers. Some of them will attend the Welsh National Eisteddfod at Treorchy, while many others will be attending the annual International Fraternal Conference of the Loyal Order of the Moose, which is being held at the City Hall, Cardiff, from July 30th. to August 1st.
>
> The P. & A. Campbell steamer, **LADY MOYRA,** will take Swansea folk, wishing to see the liner, out to the Scarweather lightvessel and accompany her up channel."

For some years attempts had been made to develop the passenger trade in Cardiff and the negotiations had, at last, come to fruition.

The 23,887 gross ton **GEORGE WASHINGTON** had been built in 1909 for the North German Lloyd Line; her American name being a marketing ploy to attract westbound passengers. She was one of about thirty German ships berthed in American ports at the outbreak of the First World War which were seized by the US authorities. The "Big George", as she was affectionately known, remained at the German liner terminal at Hoboken, New Jersey, for nearly three years until being called into active service in April 1917 by the US Navy, for troop carrying between Hoboken and Western

Europe. After the war she was taken over by the United States Lines and was chosen to carry President Woodrow Wilson and his party to and from France for the Peace Conference at Versailles in 1919.

Two Cardiff pilots boarded the liner on the morning of Sunday 29th. July 1928, to bring her up channel. The local press gave the event full coverage:-

> "Welsh-American pilgrims to the National Eisteddfod at Treorchy and members of the Loyal Order of the Moose had a striking illustration of the welcome they might expect on landing on Welsh soil, when the Lady Moyra, packed to her full complement of passengers hailing from all parts of the Swansea district, met the George Washington near the Scarweather lightship on Sunday afternoon.
>
> So extensively had announcements been made with regard to the trip that the fortunate ones were those who had booked their places some days before. There were surely 400 people in the long queue at the South Dock entrance for whom no accommodation could be provided
>
> The arrival of the George Washington had been so well timed that the passengers on the Lady Moyra received information from a man on the West Pier light-tower that the liner was visible. The gigantic vessel was near the Lightship when the Lady Moyra approached.
>
> The sun shone brilliantly, but a strong south-westerly breeze had beaten up a rather heavy swell, which had little effect on the liner, but caused some discomfort to a good many of the Lady Moyra's passengers, many of whom, from the nature of their conversation, were evidently making their first sea trip.
>
> 'Dress-ship' was the order on the liner, long strings of bunting flying from her four masts. The paddle steamer crossed the bow of the slowly moving vessel and eventually came up close on her port quarter so that the Welsh-Americans could be seen frantically waving hats and handkerchiefs.
>
> When the signal 'Welcome' was run up on the Lady Moyra's foremast, there came six blasts from the liners siren, which was the signal for an outburst of cheering from the hundreds on the pleasure boat, and responding cheers were plainly heard from the George Washington.
>
> After running alongside for some time, the liner drew ahead, but was kept within sight up to Nash Point, when the paddle steamer turned back down channel for Swansea."

Later that afternoon the other seven vessels of the Bristol Channel fleet made their way to Barry Roads to escort her; the **BRITANNIA,** from Portishead; the **CAMBRIA** and the **GLEN GOWER**, from Cardiff; the **WESTWARD HO,** from Newport and the **RAVENSWOOD,** from Clevedon and Weston. The **GLEN AVON** and **GLEN USK** also sailed from Cardiff on charter to British representatives of the Loyal Order of the Moose. They carried banners on their forward rails bearing the message "Welcome Moose"; the **GLEN GOWER,** however, stole a march on both of them by displaying a large moose head on her foremast!

All of the steamers were full to capacity and the occasion was one of the most memorable for many years. One of the newspaper reporters was particularly eloquent in his description of the warm welcome extended to the visitors:-

> "Candidly, it was an experience so happy, so colourful, so absolutely spontaneous that a rememberance of detail is as impossible as it is to recall to mind any one of the individual waves that were churned under the ships taking part.
>
> Low down on the horizon was the Somerset Coast, nearer at hand was Barry, and the coastline to Cardiff was crowded with people who looked like dolls, but whose tiny handkerchiefs fluttering in the air told that they, too, were taking part in this most novel welcome to the delegates. That perfect setting, with the George Washington in the centre of the picture, the seven Campbell steamers, so specklessly beautiful in the golden sunlight, escorting her, and the tugs and small craft that helped to fill the foreground, was all that the eye recorded.
>
> No one who was present, either on the George Washington or on the craft that crowded around her, will ever in the future quite forget that symbolic handshake on the waters."

The **GEORGE WASHINGTON** was, at that time, the largest ship to enter a Bristol Channel port. Crowds of spectators watched the 722ft. long liner squeeze into the Queen Alexandra locks. Her beam of 78ft. left a mere 6ft. clearance on each side.

The "Western Mail" concluded its report by stating:-

> "This call of the **GEORGE WASHINGTON** at Cardiff has been in the nature of an experiment; her usual route is from New York to Plymouth, Cherbourg and Bremen. But it is to be hoped that the action initiated by the United States Lines will be repeated and that they will take the wonderful appreciation which South Wales has accorded them as an inducement to consider a more permanent service."

Shortly after the **GEORGE WASHINGTON** had docked, the **GLEN GOWER** left Cardiff to meet the Cunard Liner **SCYTHIA** which arrived off Barry at 20.30 with a further party of Welsh-Americans bound for the Eisteddfod. Lining the deck of the huge vessel, they gave an inspired rendering of the Welsh National Anthem and the ever popular hymns "Cwm Rhondda" and "Aberystwyth". The **SCYTHIA** was boarded by the Lord Mayor of Cardiff and sundry dignitaries, some of whom arrived straight from the **GEORGE WASHINGTON,** to extend their second official welcome of the day. One of the visitors presented the Eisteddfod Secretary with a Welsh flag, flown by the **SCYTHIA** during the voyage, which was destined to flutter over the Treorchy pavilion for the duration of the Eisteddfod.

Such occasions were great "money spinners" for the steamers; the takings from the **GEORGE WASHINGTON** and **SCYTHIA** cruises alone were approximately £1380, a considerable sum in those days! Further revenue was earned by the **RAVENSWOOD** on the following morning when she was chartered to act as tender to the **SCYTHIA,** landing 637 of her passengers in the Queen Alexandra Dock, Cardiff, on their way to attend the festivities at the Welsh valley town.

The satisfactory season was followed, however, by tragedy. On Monday 10th. December 1928, Capt. Alec Campbell died at his home, Ferngrove, in Kilmun. He was aged 66, and had been joint Managing Director with his brother since the company's inception. On their arrival in Bristol, Alec and Peter met with considerable opposition from the rival shipping companies and their partisans. Nevertheless, they remained resolute and ran their company with great efficiency, eventually becoming the sole operators of excursion steamers in the Bristol Channel. Alec, very much the business brain behind the organisation, steered the company through the difficult years as well as taking command of a number of the steamers. He was a superb seaman and his quiet, genial nature endeared him to all who knew him. In 1914 he had set up home again in his beloved Scotland but travelled south to Bristol at the start of each season. In latter years he had become very frail and, in fact, suffered from serious heart trouble. His funeral took place on Thursday 13th. December and he was buried at Kilmun.

The passenger liner traffic at Cardiff attained prominence early in 1929. On the afternoon of Saturday 6th. April the **BRITANNIA** and the **GLEN AVON** escorted the Canadian Pacific liner, **MONTROSE.**

The **GLEN AVON** met the Cunard liner, **ALAUNIA,** off Lavernock Point on Saturday 27th. April, and the **RAVENSWOOD,** once again, acted as tender, taking 307 emigrants from the Queen Alexandra Dock to board the liner anchored off Flat Holm.

The **MONTROSE** called again on Saturday 4th. May, with the **GLEN USK** in attendance, and on Saturday 25th. May the **MINNEDOSA'S** arrival was witnessed by capacity crowds aboard the **RAVENSWOOD, GLEN AVON** and **GLEN GOWER.**

The **LADY MOYRA** had entered service at Whitsun and, on Saturday 8th. June, during Swansea Regatta week, ran several cruises to view the international racing yachts, **SHAMROCK, WHITE HEATHER, LULWORTH** and **CAMBRIA,** competing in races in Swansea Bay. Full details of the events appeared in the Swansea newspapers, including the following, rather embarrassing report under the headline, "The Lady Moyra causes an Incident.":-

"From our Yachting Correspondent on the Official Committee Boat. The yachts were due to start their race at 11.00. At 10.50 a preparatory gun was fired and the yachts approached the starting line. At 10.55. the five minute gun was fired and a few minutes later an extraordinary incident happened - The Lady Moyra, with a big crowd of passengers aboard, actually steamed in front of the yachts as they were lined up. The racing officials were wild, and Mr. Le Boulanger, the acting committee secretary, took up his speaking trumpet and told the master what he thought of him! However, the passenger boat passed along in time."

What a pity "Our Yachting Correspondent" did not elaborate on Mr. Le Boulanger's comments, but they were probably unprintable.

The **DEVONIA** left Cardiff and Ilfracombe, to join the **WAVERLEY** and **BRIGHTON BELLE** on the South Coast, on Friday 21st. June. Later in the day the Downend Watchouse reported that she was seen drifting up channel, in Bideford Bay, two miles off Baggy Point. This somewhat unusual incident baffled the coastguard but she was not in danger. She had simply stopped for engine repairs and was under way again after about two hours.

On Friday 2nd. August the **LADY MOYRA** was involved in a "rescue mission". The Swansea press reported:-

> "Passengers from Swansea on Friday afternoon's trip of the Lady Moyra to Ilfracombe saw their vessel converted into a "rescue" ship, when they were near their journey's end.
>
> Spectators on Ilfracombe Pier, who were looking out for the Swansea boat, were puzzled by the zig-zag course she appeared to be steering. Then it was noticed that the Cambria, which had left at 16.00 with a large complement of passengers for Barry, Clevedon and Avonmouth, had dropped anchor near Rillage Point.
>
> The Lady Moyra was seen to be bearing down on her and, as she cruised near her, everyone wondered what was going to happen next. Presently the Lady Moyra made for Ilfracombe Pier and it then transpired that she had picked up a radio message from the Cambria, while crossing from Swansea, and that while the steamer was in no danger, she was unable to move owing to paddle trouble.
>
> Having discharged her Swansea passengers the Lady Moyra went out and took the Cambria in tow: onlookers were given a fine example of clever manoeuvring by Capt. Riddell which resulted in a rope being passed aboard the Cambria's stern. She was then towed, very slowly, astern and berthed at the pier.
>
> The Lady Moyra, which was due out of Ilfracombe at 17.00, was delayed for two hours and then took aboard the Cambria's passengers with the object of their catching the train which left Swansea, High Street, at 21.10. (No call was made at Mumbles Pier). The trippers landed in Swansea a few minutes before 21.00 and there was an exciting dash in taxis and other conveyances to the station.
>
> The Lady Moyra does not, as a rule, sail on Fridays but made a special journey this time for the benefit of the Bank Holiday trippers."

The **CAMBRIA** left Ilfracombe, for Cardiff, at 04.00 on Saturday 3rd. August and made two runs on the ferry before making her way to Bristol for permanent repairs to be carried out to her damaged paddle on the following day.

The **CAMBRIA** featured in the headlines again when, on the evening of Thursday 5th. September, she was fogbound off Porthcawl and caused considerable alarm in certain quarters. To quote the Swansea press once more:-

> "A thick bank of fog which crept up the Bristol Channel at dusk on Thursday evening was responsible for keeping the Mumbles lifeboat at sea all night.
>
> On Friday morning she returned to her station, twelve hours after she had put out, unnecessarily as it transpired, to assist the P. & A. Campbell passenger

steamer, Cambria, which, just before reaching Porthcawl, had been forced by the impenetrability of the fog, to drop anchor.

The steamer, from Ilfracombe, had 200 passengers to land at Porthcawl and was due in at 19.45; the remainder of her complement were bound for Barry. It was about 20.00 when she ran into the fog bank off Rest Bay and dropped anchor a few hundred yards from the shore.

People at the Royal Porthcawl Golf Club saw her masthead light and informed the coastguard station. Officers there telephoned for the Mumbles lifeboat which was launched in the presence of thousands of holidaymakers who had gathered on the pier to see a firework display.

The Chief Coastguard communicated with the Cambria by means of morse signals on the powerful headlamps of Mr. Franklin Thomas's motor car. Capt. Bernard Hawken signalled in reply that his ship was in no danger and that he was waiting for the fog to lift before coming into Porthcawl. The Cambria reached the breakwater and landed her passengers at about 21.30, the captain and crew being loudly cheered by onlookers and all those on board. Shortly after, she left for Barry.

In Swansea Bay, the fog persisted and although informed that her services were not required, the lifeboat was unable to regain her boat house, at the pier, until this morning."

The summer weather was reasonably good and passenger figures were satisfactory. The **GLEN GOWER** visited Newquay, from Cardiff, on Sunday 11th. August, and on the following day the **BRITANNIA** made a day return trip, also from Cardiff, to Milford Haven. She ran a cruise from the Pembokeshire port with 900 passengers, leaving 400 behind. On Sunday 1st. September she visited West Wales again, this time running a day return trip from Milford Haven to Ilfracombe.

The South Coast season had also been satisfactory. The **DEVONIA** ran an interesting excursion on Saturday 7th. September when she sailed from Brighton to the Solent, where she anchored off Calshot to witness the 10th. Annual Schneider Trophy Race, for seaplanes. Her passengers saw the first of three successive wins for Great Britain when it was won by an RAF Supermarine S6.

The **DEVONIA** and **BRIGHTON BELLE** accomplished their round trips to Bristol eneventfully, but the **WAVERLEY** was not so fortunate. She left Brighton on the morning of Monday 7th. October. A gale warning was received that evening and at 20.30 she was battling through heavy seas when Capt. William Bruford considered it advisable to shelter in Torbay. She weighed anchor at 05.00 on the following day. Heavy seas damaged one of her sponson doors but she proceeded and rounded Land's End at 13.40. The gale had now veered to the north and at 15.00, having just passed Pendeen Watch, conditions were so bad that she was forced to put about and anchor in Mount's Bay at 17.30. On the morning of Wednesday 9th. October she entered Penzance harbour to take on water and anchored offshore again at about mid-day. By late afternoon the wind had moderated and she proceeded, but still had to contend with heavy, confused seas. She arrived off Ilfracombe at 01.00 on the following day but was unable to berth, because of the heavy weather, until 03.00. She eventually arrived at Bristol at 10.00 on Thursday 10th. October.

With the 1929 season over the decade drew to its close. In retrospect the years since the Great War had not been easy. The company's business was so dependent on the weather and in the past eleven seasons, only four had produced what could be termed "good" summers in terms of passenger figures. In addition, the coal strikes, the General Strike and rising unemployment all conspired to inflict further damage to the company's operations. October 1929 had brought the Wall Street Crash, and, although far from home, the predicament of the American economy was to have repercussions throughout the whole of Western Europe.

However, the British people, with their customary resilience and their capacity for "making the most of it", rose above the gloom and despondency in their determination to enjoy themselves. The atmosphere of the time is exemplified by Mr. E.C.B. Thornton in his book, "South Coast Pleasure Steamers". On taking his first job in SW London he became very well acquainted with the White Funnel steamers at Brighton, with the aid of a motor cycle:-

> "Well does the writer recall riding to Brighton and embarking on the Brighton Belle for a cruise to Eastbourne and back. The ship passed the Devonia between the piers at Brighton and she looked splendid. He instituted a system, two or three times a year as funds permitted, of motor biking to Brighton, pushing the machine into a garage and a bag into an hotel and going on the Devonia for her Saturday afternoon trip, usually to Ventnor, Ryde or Shanklin, but sometimes to Hastings."

DEVONIA at Eastbourne. 1929. (HAA)

Swansea Regatta Week. The RAVENSWOOD arrives at Mumbles Pier in the late 1920's. (CCC)

Ilfracombe Regatta Week 1928, with the CAMBRIA arriving from Cardiff. The steamer offshore was as much a part of Ilfracombe as the White Funnel Fleet. She was built in 1893 and carried coal from the South Wales ports to the harbour for the Ilfracombe Gas Company and local coal merchants. She was painted black and was always covered with a liberal coating of coal dust. With characteristic West Country humour, her owners, the Irwin family of Combe Martin, named her "SNOWFLAKE". (HGO)

Sea-planes visit Ilfracombe. The LADY MOYRA lies at the face of the pier. 1920's. (CCC)

The arrival of the GEORGE WASHINGTON at Cardiff, Sunday 29th. July 1928, escorted by the GLEN USK. (CCC)

The "Big George" seen from the GLEN USK. The GLEN GOWER, with the moose head on her foremast, appears from behind the liner's starboard bow. (CCC)

The GEORGE WASHINGTON approaches the Queen Alexandra dock entrance with, (L to R), the WESTWARD HO, GLEN AVON, RAVENSWOOD and CAMBRIA. (CCC)

Capt. Henry Chidgey and Chief Officer Jack Wide on the bridge of the GLEN AVON. Late 1920's. (ERK)

Capt. George Spong on the bridge of the GLEN USK. (ERK)

P. & A. Campbell Ltd.   **WHITE FUNNEL FLEET**

Special . . .      Special . . .
Attractions.   Attractions.

Messrs. P. & A. CAMPBELL, Ltd., Magnificent Saloon Steamers

'Britannia,' 'Glen Gower,' 'Glen Usk,' etc.

Will (Weather and circumstances permitting) run the following EXCURSIONS:—

CHEAP CIRCULAR

FRIDAY,
Sept. 27th

Evening Cruise to Minehead & Barry

(Not to land) and Back.

Leaving Ilfracombe 5-20 p.m.,
arriving back about 10-15 p.m.   **Cheap Fare. 2/-**

Special Attraction at Cardiff. Rugby Football Match—CARDIFF v. SKEWIN

Cheap End of Season Day Trip to

Penarth, Cardiff
Clevedon and Bristol

SATURDAY,

Leaving Ilfracombe **8-45** a.m.
Returning from Bristol 3-45 p.m., Clevedon 4-45, Cardiff 5-45, Penarth 5-55, direct
for Ilfracombe.

Sept. 28th

RETURN FARES :

To Penarth or Cardiff **5/-** Clevedon or Bristol **6/-**

NOTE—Providing there are sufficient Passengers the National Bus Co., Ltd., will
operate a Service leaving Barnstaple 7-30 a.m., Braunton 7-50, Foxhunters 8-10,
for Ilfracombe Pier. The Bus will depart from the Pier on arrival of the
steamer at night.
Convenient Services from and to Combe Martin. Usual Fares.

Single Trip to Newport (direct).
Leaving Ilfracombe 9-50 p.m.
Steamer leaves Newport for Ilfracombe 3-30 p.m. SINGLE FARE 6/-

Breakfasts, Dinners, Teas, etc., Served on Board at **Moderate Prices**

CHILDREN UNDER 14 HALF-PRICE.

For further particulars apply to the Agents—   F W. BIRMINGHAM, 10 The Quay, Ilfracombe.
                                                     G. S. RICHARDS, Office. Esplanade. Lynmouth.
                                                     B. WEBSTER, 12 Cross Street, Barnstaple.
Telephones—158 ILFRACOMBE.   14 LYNTON   P. & A. CAMPBELL LTD., Britannia Buildings,
          3112 BRISTOL.   Cumberland Basin, Bristol

Bruce Moore, "Chronicle & Gazette" Press, Ilfracombe.

Ilfracombe timetable, 1929.

The GLEN USK arriving at Ilfracombe early in the 1929 season. The flags are at half-mast following the death of Capt. Alec. (HGO)

Barry Regatta Week in the late 1920's. The RAVENSWOOD lies at the pier while the Barry lifeboat returns with passengers after a "trip around the bay" and a Newport pilot cutter awaits her next turn of duty. (ERK)

The GLEN USK and LADY MOYRA at the Stone Bench, Ilfracombe in 1929. (HGO)

A blast on the whistle as the WESTWARD HO leaves Hotwells Landing Stage, Bristol, in 1929. (ERK)

Passengers aboard the GLEN USK arriving at Ilfracombe in the 1920's.

Passengers aboard the DEVONIA at Ilfracombe in the 1920's. (CCC)

The DEVONIA at Bournemouth Pier in the 1920's. (CCC)

Aboard the DEVONIA in the Solent on Schneider Trophy Day. Saturday 7th. September 1929. (HAA)

The WESTWARD HO arriving at Mumbles, 1929. (HGO)

A lunchtime arrival at Ilfracombe for the GLEN GOWER. She is en route from Cardiff, Penarth, Barry, Minehead and Lynmouth to Clovelly. (HGO)

Spot the differences! The CAMBRIA and BRITANNIA arriving at Ilfracombe in 1929. Sister-ships but not identical.
(HGO)

Chapter 5 – 1930/1931

Following the death of Alec Campbell, Capt. Peter, then aged 70, remained as Joint Managing Director; his new associate was Mr. William James Banks, who had joined the Board of Directors in May 1926. Both men possessed considerable engineering skills but, perhaps, lacked Alec's astute business acumen

It has been asserted that, during the 1930's, the company stagnated to some extent. This criticism is, however, somewhat harsh considering the financial climate of the time; indeed, the fact that the company survived the difficult early years of the decade is surely a reflection of sound management.

The passenger liner trade at Cardiff did not flourish to the degree hoped for but nevertheless provided a welcome source of revenue for the steamers.

The **RAVENSWOOD** was once again engaged on her tendering duties, during the weekend before the 1930 season began. She took 91 emigrants from the Queen Alexandra Dock, Cardiff, on Saturday 29th. March, to board the Cunard liner, **AUSONIA,** at anchor in Barry Roads. The memorandum book records that the captain of the liner complimented Capt. Brander on the capable way in which he brought the **RAVENSWOOD** alongside.

On the following day the White Star liner, **MEGANTIC,** anchored in Barry Roads. While the **RAVENSWOOD** was alongside her that evening, cries of "Man overboard" were heard. A customs officer, conducting a party of visitors over the liner, had opened a door in the ship's side by mistake and had fallen twenty feet into the sea. The **RAVENSWOOD** immediately cast off and searched for him, in company with other small craft, but, unfortunately, the customs officer was not found.

She tendered the Cunard liner, **ALAUNIA,** on Saturday 26th. April and the memorandum book records that the charge for this service was £90 0s 0d plus £2 10s 0d for baggage handling by the crew.

The **RAVENSWOOD** was in trouble on the morning of Thursday 5th. June. She had anchored overnight in Penarth Roads and on making her way into Cardiff, ran aground on the shingle beach below Penarth Head. Fortunately, the **GLEN AVON** had just left Cardiff on her first ferry crossing; Capt. Chidgey took her close inshore and towed the **RAVENSWOOD** off. The latter proceeded straight to Bristol, where an inspection showed that she had sustained only slight damage to her starboard paddle and, after repairs, re-entered service on the following day.

Early in the year the Admiralty had arranged a series of courtesy visits by warships to various ports and resorts, as part of the Atlantic Fleet's programme of summer cruises. To coincide with Barry Regatta Week a flotilla of five destroyers, including their flagship, **HMS WALLACE,** anchored in Barry Roads on Monday 9th. June and, as usual, several of the steamers ran cruises to view the warships over the following couple of days.

Similar cruises took place on the South Coast during the following month, when a number of warships, including the cruisers **YORK, HAWKINS** and **FROBISHER,** were at anchor off Brighton.

On the morning of Sunday 3rd. August the **LADY MOYRA** sailed from Swansea and Mumbles to meet the Cunard liner, **LACONIA,** bringing a party of Welsh-Americans to attend the National Eisteddfod at Llanelly. The liner was late and did not, in fact, arrive in Swansea Bay until late afternoon. Fortunately the **LADY MOYRA'S** passengers were not disappointed, Capt. Riddell took his ship to the Helwick Lightvessel, from where she escorted the White Star liner, **BALTIC,** up the coast to off Mumbles Head. The **BALTIC,** also arriving from America with passengers for the Eisteddfod, was bound for Barry Roads, where she arrived at 15.00 to be met by the **BRITANNIA, CAMBRIA, WESTWARD HO, GLEN AVON** and **GLEN GOWER.** The **RAVENSWOOD,** once again, tendered the liner and sailed to meet her with guests of the White Star Line.

After her cruise to meet the **BALTIC,** the **BRITANNIA** landed her passengers at Clevedon and anchored offshore to await the tide at Bristol. While proceeding up the river, at 03.45 next day she struck the stone Hotwells slip and damaged four floats in her port paddle wheel. However, the ends of the floats were cut off and she was able to continue with her scheduled sailings, permanent repairs being carried out during the following winter.

On the morning of Saturday 23rd. August the **LADY MOYRA** made her usual return crossing from Swansea to Ilfracombe, but about mid-day the Bristol Channel was struck by a severe gale which blew up from the south west. She left Swansea at 15.20 for Mumbles and Ilfracombe but was forced to put back off the Scarweather Lightvessel after heavy seas had smashed two of her large, after saloon windows and damaged her forward starboard rail. A successful, but very lively crossing was made later in the evening which left Ilfracombe at 22.55. She had to anchor off Mumbles for a few hours to await the tide and berthed at Swansea a little after 04.00 on the following morning. The broken windows, which had been boarded up, were replaced on her next off service day. The large windows were always particularly vulnerable and during the following winter they were reduced in size, as they had been on her sister ship, the **DEVONIA,** after the war.

Some of the more unusual sailings that year were the **BRITANNIA'S** day trip from Cardiff and Penarth to Porthcawl, Mumbles, Tenby and Pembroke Dock, with a cruise, on Sunday 13th. July, and the charter of the **GLEN USK** and **GLEN GOWER** from Briton Ferry on Saturday 13th. September. They had been scheduled to sail to Tenby for the day but, owing to unfavourable weather, a much shorter trip, to Mumbles, had to be substituted.

The South Coast sailings proceeded without incident until Saturday 23rd. August. The **BRIGHTON BELLE,** after lying at anchor off Brighton overnight, was making her way to Eastbourne to begin her day's work when her master, Capt. J. Gilmore, sighted a motor yacht flying her ensign upside down, about two miles off Beachy Head. The distress signal was answered by the **BRIGHTON BELLE** which took the yacht, the **FIREFLY**, disabled owing to engine failure, in tow to Newhaven.

One of the worst round trips from Brighton to Bristol was experienced by the **DEVONIA** at the end of the season. Capt. Couves, never a man to turn back or seek shelter, brought her through ferocious conditions but not without her sustaining considerable damage. The memorandum book entries, taken from the ship's log, are fully quoted:-

"Friday 26th. September 1930.
14.32. Left Palace Pier, Brighton.
21.00. Sea unshipped port forward lifeboat.
        Vessel straining heavily.
        Damage to hull unknown.
22.00. Stopped for engine purposes.
24.00. Start Point. Fresh northerly gale & sea.

Saturday 27th. September 1930.
05.55. Passed Longships.
06.00. Half speed.
06.10. Slow speed. Mountainous seas. Ship taking heavy water on board.
06.15. Heavy sea unshipped starboard lifeboat. Also stove in port forward wing.
07.00. Pendeen Watch.
08.00. Strong NE gale and heavy, mountainous seas.
        Ship labouring heavily under stress of weather. Starboard lifeboat stove in.
11.07. Trevose Head abeam.
11.30. Shipped heavy seas breaking 3 ports in port and starboard wings.
15.14. Hartland Point abeam. Wind and sea moderating. Proceeded at full speed.
17.15. Left Ilfracombe.
21.30. Arrived at Bristol pontoon, then into basin.
        Examination on arrival found sundry deck damage.
        Damage to hull unknown."

The Directors report for the year made depressing reading and stated:

"The company showed a profit of £4463, making with £2784 brought forward, an available balance of £7247. The directors have provided £895 for depreciation, £1406 for preference dividend, £400 for fees, and propose to carry the balance of £4546 forward. The directors regret the unfortunate result of the year's trading. This, however, must be attributed entirely to the bad weather which prevailed from the middle of July to the end of September."

A number of intriguing questions hang over the end of the year, arising from an entry in the Minute Book for Wednesday 24th. December:-

"Capt. Peter reported that a representative of Cosens would inspect the steamer on Monday 29th. December 1930. The purchase price put forward being £10,000."

The steamer in question was the **BRIGHTON BELLE** and Cosens & Co. were pleasure steamer owners, based in Weymouth. The matter poses several queries:- Was the proposal instigated by Campbell's and, if so, was it put forward because the company had too many ships? Did they consider the **BRIGHTON BELLE** to be surplus, or were they forced into trying to raise more capital because of the poor trading figures? Or did the proposition originate with Cosens? Did any negotiations actually take place; £10,000 would appear to have been a somewhat excessive price to ask; did Cosens consider it too high? Could it be that Campbell's were not desperate to sell the ship but were simply testing the market and therefore were prepared to hold out for their price on an "all or nothing" basis

The Cosens specialist, Mr. Richard Clammer, states that the matter of the **BRIGHTON BELLE** is something of a mystery in that no mention appears in the Cosens minute books at all. It is therefore not possible to say with certainty who instigated the inspection but the man responsible was probably Frederick Jones, Cosens joint manager and marine superintendent, who had for many years been trying to talk the board into obtaining a new vessel.

In November 1930 Cosens **ALEXANDRA** failed her survey and during the following month was advertised for sale. Thus, Cosens were one ship short and may have been seeking a replacement medium-distance vessel of a more modern design. The **ALEXANDRA** was very old-fashioned with her open foredeck and narrow after saloon, therefore the **BRIGHTON BELLE** might have seemed an ideal replacement.

No further details can be ascertained and the matter must end on an inconclusive note but, whatever the reasons behind the proposition, no such sale took place. Neither company, it appears, considered the transaction particularly pressing; the **BRIGHTON BELLE** remained in Campbell's ownership until the end of her career, and Cosens did not add to their fleet until 1937.

1931 can only be described as the most abysmal season of the decade! It was one of the worst years of the depression and the summer weather was deplorable, with short, fine spells few and far between.

The season began with a disaster. On the evening of Saturday 28th. March, during the weekend before Easter, several cargo vessels were at anchor in Lundy Roads when the SW gale, from which they were sheltering, suddenly backed to the SE and caught them unawares. They all managed to clear the island except the Greek steamer, **TAXIARCHIS,** outward bound from Cardiff to Rosario with over 4000 tons of coal and coke, which dragged her anchors and was driven ashore on the cliffs below the quarry on the eastern side of the island. She had two holds flooded but otherwise held together, her entire crew having been taken ashore, without injury, by way of the Lundy life saving apparatus.

The misfortune of one vessel, however, was of benefit to others. On many of their timetables P. & A. Campbell Ltd. advised potential passengers of the opportunity to see the **TAXIARCHIS** ashore and passenger figures on the Lundy trips increased as a consequence.

The steamer remained ashore for over two years until, somewhat unexpectedly in view of previous unsuccessful attempts, she was refloated and towed, despite a bad list to starboard, into Ilfracombe harbour, by a local salvage company. She was beyond repair, however, and was later broken up.

The South Coast sailings were once again taken by the **WAVERLEY, BRIGHTON BELLE** and **DEVONIA.** Capt. William Bruford took the **WAVERLEY** around at Easter but she was cancelled for ten consecutive days in mid-April owing to the cold and windy weather discouraging all but a minimum of hardy, potential passengers. She had the distinction of running the first post-war trip to Shanklin, Isle of Wight, on Saturday 23rd. May before being joined by the **BRIGHTON BELLE,** under the temporary command of Capt. Couves, during the following week. In mid-June the **BRIGHTON BELLE** was taken over by Capt. E. Smith, allowing Bill Couves to take the **DEVONIA** south for the rest of the season.

Among the regular passengers on the White Funnel steamers since the 1930's were Miss Gwyneth White, and her late brother, Gwilym, of Penarth. Now in her mid-80's, this lady has very kindly given permission for the publication of extracts from her sailing diaries. Her eye for detail and her eloquent narrative style enliven even the most commonplace of sailings, and provide a fascinating insight into those aspects of the trips which were once taken so much for granted, but which now remain no more than fond memories:-

"Sunday 28th. June 1931.
Gwilym and I went for a channel cruise this evening, on the Glen Avon. It was a cheap trip, 1/6d., inclusive of the pier toll and there was a very large crowd at Penarth, while the boat was already well filled with Cardiff passengers. We went down to the Breaksea Lightship, off Barry, where parcels of newspapers, books and magazines were put on board for her crew. It was a lovely evening with a very calm sea and we came back around the Steep and Flat Holms, going very close in to both of them, before returning to Penarth at about 9pm after a trip of two hours."

The practice of passing parcels to the lightvessels was undertaken at the English & Welsh Grounds, the Breaksea and the Scarweather but could only be accomplished in calm weather; one or two of the lightship's crew would row out to the steamer, standing a little way off, and the parcels were transferred from the after sponson.

On the following weekend the Whites were afloat again, this time for a special occasion:-

"Sunday 5th. July 1931.
Our boat trip this afternoon took us to visit the battleship, Malaya, which was lying two miles off Weston Super Mare, in the direction of Brean Down. There was a bigger crowd on Penarth pier than I have ever seen, nearly 400. The steamer, the Glen Usk, was already packed with Cardiffians but we managed to squeeze on board. We were off the Malaya in half an hour but had to wait for about twenty minutes while the Lady Moyra, from Swansea, disembarked her passengers on to the battleship. Then came our turn and, after us, the Glen Avon and innumerable launches from Weston. The combined passengers from all these vessels taxed even the capacity of the warship; in fact I heard many of her crew saying that they had never expected such a crowd. After a three hour tour of the Malaya, the Glen Avon was the first boat to leave but many of her passengers missed her so, after the Lady Moyra had departed with her full

complement for Minehead, Porthcawl and Swansea, the master of the Glen Usk, Capt. Edward Calvert, agreed to take the stranded Weston passengers home, even thought it was not part of her schedule. Campbells must have done very well indeed out of these trips for, in addition to those steamers which actually visited the Malaya, several others cruised around her and were very well patronised."

The occasional sailings to Newquay, which had taken place since the 1900's, were terminated at the end of 1930, and visits to Padstow were substituted from 1931. The first such trip took place on Sunday 12th. July when the **LADY MOYRA** sailed from Swansea, Mumbles and Ilfracombe, with a connection provided from Cardiff and Penarth. Once again the Whites were aboard:-

"We left Penarth at 7.30am aboard the Glen Gower and changed to the Lady Moyra at Ilfracombe, which had brought a good crowd over from Swansea. The sun was shining when we left at 10.30 but between Morte Point and Hartland we had a succession of showers. However, by the time we passed Bude the sun was blazing down on the glorious blue sea, of a hue of which Cornwall alone can boast. We passed Boscastle and Tintagel before rounding Pentire Head, just after two-o-clock, and sailing up the estuary of the River Camel to Padstow."

The reason behind the change of destination is best summed up by quoting Miss White's final sentence:-

"The greater part of the population of the district were waiting on the quay to go for the cruise around Trevose Head and down the coast to off Newquay."

The journey to Padstow took about an hour less than that to Newquay and, as landing was accomplished at the jetty, the timing allowed for a cruise to be made from the Cornish port, usually to off Newquay, and which, more often than not, was very well patronised. Although the total steaming distance was about the same, the Padstow cruise passengers would naturally provide a welcome increase in the day's takings. The landing and re-embarking at Newquay, being performed by small boats, left no time for an extending cruise and the opportunity for further revenue was missed. Sound economic sense therefore prevailed, rendered all the more necessary in the financial climate of the time.

The question is frequently asked why passengers were landed by boat at Newquay when the harbour was large enough to accommodate the steamers, particularly at the north jetty. The answer is, again, simply one of finance; the landing dues imposed by the owners of the harbour, the Great Western Railway, were considered excessive and the company was not prepared to pay them!

Some of the sailings to Padstow were more of an "endurance test" than a day trip, for both passengers and crew! For example, on Monday 10th. August the **BRITANNIA** left Bristol at 05.15 for Cardiff, Minehead, Lynmouth and Ilfracombe, arriving at Padstow at 15.00. After the cruise down the coast she left at 17.00 and returned to Ilfracombe, where she remained for the night. Her passengers transferred to the **GLEN GOWER** which left Ilfracombe at 21.15, Minehead at 23.15, Cardiff at 01.15 on the following day, eventually arriving at Bristol at 03.20. Quite a day out! The passengers, after their 22 hour trip, could then, of course, go home to bed: not so for the crew of the **GLEN GOWER**. At 04.20 she made her way, light, to Avonmouth, leaving there three hours later bound for Barry and the start of another day's work.

Another occasional sailing revived in 1931, after a lapse of several years, was that to Porlock. The **LADY MOYRA** made the only two trips that year when she sailed to the Somerset village,from Swansea, via Porthcawl and Lynmouth, on Friday 14th. August and Tuesday 1st. September.

One of the most unfortunate incidents to occur in the Bristol Channel for many years was the near destruction of Penarth Pier on the evening of Bank Holiday Monday 3rd. August. In the old pavilion at the end of the pier, a discarded cigarette, not fully extinguished, was the most likely cause of debris under the floorboards beginning to smoulder. At 21.00 fire broke out and within an hour the pavilion collapsed in flames. The fire spread along the wooden planking, destroyed the two shelters and, at 23.00, caused the central portion of the pier to collapse into the sea. Over 500 spectators lined the seafront to watch the inferno until, at about midnight, it burned itself out. Although a number of people sustained minor injuries, miraculously there were no fatalities. The pier, naturally, took some time to repair but the steamer trips were cancelled for only about two weeks, during which time temporary planking was fixed over the collapsed portion, enabling passengers to reach the landing stage in safety. Sailings were resumed on Saturday 15th. August.

On the following morning gales once again swept across the southern half of the country. Gwyneth and Gwilym White set off from Penarth on the **GLEN GOWER,** bound for Tenby, via Minehead, Lynmouth, and Ilfracombe. They did not reach their destination: Miss White tells the story:

> "After leaving Minehead it began to get quite choppy and we kept further out than I can remember. The wind became much stronger and spindrift was whipped off the waves and rose up the cliff side. Near Ilfracombe we rolled considerably, deck chairs were blown around and several people lost their hats. We reached Ilfracombe just before 1300 and then were told that there would be no crossing to Tenby owing to the gale....
>
> We walked to Lee Bay and, while eating our lunch on the cliff top, saw the **BRITANNIA,** which had come down from Bristol behind us, pass below us on her way out to Lundy. We were very surprised, never expecting her to attempt it. She ventured no further than Morte Point, however, and had to turn back. The whole channel was a mass of white crested waves, and at Bull Point, the storm cone was hoisted....
>
> We left Ilfracombe at 19.45; backing out of the harbour, the wind caught us under the stern and we pitched and tossed greatly, and although we had the gale behind us, for the first half hour we scarcely seemed to make any progress at all, but after Lynmouth speed improved.
>
> At Minehead, to our surprise, the tide was so high that the top platform of the pier was awash so we had to put in to the old stone jetty, where a good deal of time was lost manoeuvring into a favourable position. We heard later that not all those who had disembarked in the morning could regain the jetty, owing to the flooding of the promenade by the abnormal tide."

This most unusual occurrence formed part of an article in the "Western Mail" next morning:-

Remarkable scenes were witnessed at Minehead on Sunday night when mountainous seas rushed over the esplanade, marooning people and trippers from Wales, and flooding roads, fields, refreshment tents and bathing huts.

Scores of people who watched the high seas were surrounded by the water which rushed into the neighbouring roads and fields. Girls who had taken refuge in a shelter had to be carried out. Passengers in the pleasure steamer Glen Gower could not be disembarked at the pier owing to the highest landing stage being under water and the vessel was taken into the tiny harbour...

August continued her inglorious course during the weekend and the hope of a belated summer is still deferred. Features of the weekend weather were high winds, thunderstorms and heavy rain. In most places it was the twenty-seventh wet weekend this year. Once more the weather was the despair of promoters of outdoor events. How many this summer have had their desired conditions?

A number of bathing machines, canoes and deck chairs were washed away on both Saturday and Sunday nights at Tenby as a result of the exceedingly high tide on the north beach."

The article then went on to give details of the disruption which the weather caused in other parts of the country, including the south coast:-

"Two people were injured, one narrowly escaping drowning, when tidal waves swept over Worthing beach on Sunday afternoon. Six enormous waves crashed on to the beach in quick succession, sending bathers rushing up the stones for safety."

The three south coast steamers were, in fact, stormbound in Newhaven on that, and the following day.

Bad weather was also responsible for the postponement of the Schneider Trophy Air Race on Saturday 12th. September. The **DEVONIA** had sailed from Brighton to Spithead to witness the event but was back at Brighton by late afternoon. The race was, however, held on the following day and, after a hasty re-scheduling of trips, the **WAVERLEY** was in attendance.

Having completed her season, the **BRIGHTON BELLE** left Newhaven for Bristol at 23.45 on Monday 14th. September. A few days later the following paragraph appeared in a Bristol newspaper:-

"Despite an all-night search by the St. Mary's (Land's End) lifeboat, no trace was found yesterday of a vessel which had flown distress signals five miles off the Longships Lighthouse on Tuesday afternoon. It was feared yesterday morning that the vessel might have been the pleasure steamer Brighton Belle, but the vessel docked safely later in the day at Bristol."

The memorandum book, however, clarifies the situation:-

"Tuesday 15th. September 1931.

Brighton Belle. 17.00. Observed following signal flying on Longships 'Want immediate assistance'. Wireless message sent to Land's End radio - assistance sent - proceeded."

The Bristol Channel services that season had been particularly badly affected by the depression. The Welsh valleys covered a massive area of South Wales and were densely populated by a community, most of whom were involved in the production of coal and its allied industries. Many of the collieries were closed completely and most others were on short time working, throwing many people out of work. A large percentage of that community would otherwise have been a valuable source of revenue for the company but passenger figures from Cardiff and Swansea were considerably reduced.

The financial report stated that the company had the unique experience of sustaining a loss and appended the following table illustrating the results of the past five years:-

Year	Profit	Loss
1927	£16,966	—
1928	£26,578	—
1929	£24,711	—
1930	£4,463	—
1931	—	£2,686

In an attempt to redress the balance of this predicament the company considered, among other proposals, a new field of enterprise. Capt. Dan Taylor was asked to look into the viability of running a steamer on the South Devon Coast.

The WESTWARD HO rolls into Ilfracombe Pier in 1931. (CCC)

P. & A. CAMPBELL LTD.

BARRY REGATTA

Tuesday, June 10th, 1930

(Weather and circumstances permitting)

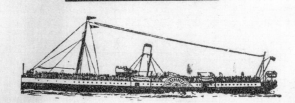

SPECIAL CRUISE

To view H.M.S. "WALLACE" and Flotilla of Destroyers.

Leave Barry Pier at 12.30 p.m., back about 1.45 p.m.

Fare 1/-

For Further Particulars apply to

WM. GUY, 1, STUART STREET, CARDIFF; OR

P. & A. CAMPBELL LTD., CUMBERLAND BASIN, BRISTOL.

Dates, Ltd., Printers, Docks, Cardiff

The BRITANNIA arriving at Swansea on the evening of Saturday 16th. August 1930, in readiness for her following day's sailing to West Wales. (HGO)

The timetable for the BRITANNIA'S cruise to the Pembrokeshire Islands.

The BRITANNIA returns to Milford Haven after her cruise around Skokholm and Skomer. Sunday 17th. August 1930. (HGO)

Capt. Findlay Brander manoeuvres the RAVENSWOOD out of the Queen Alexandra Dock, Cardiff, taking her complement of emigrants to board the Cunard liner, AUSONIA, anchored in Barry Roads. Saturday 29th. March 1930. (CCC)

The RAVENSWOOD approaches the White Star liner, BALTIC, off Barry, Sunday 3rd. August 1930.

The DEVONIA in Newhaven harbour. 1930. (HGO)

Southern and Great Western Railways and P. & A. Campbell Ltd.

SPECIAL EXCURSION

From Brighton, Worthing, Eastbourne and Hastings

TO ILFRACOMBE, CARDIFF & BRISTOL

(Weather and circumstances permitting), by the Magnificent Saloon Steamer

"DEVONIA"

On Friday, Sept. 26th, 1930

Leaving Brighton (Palace Pier) at 2.30 p.m., due to arrive at Ilfracombe about 2 p.m. on Saturday, 27th, and leave Ilfracombe at 5 p.m., arriving at Bristol about 9.15 p.m. Passengers to Cardiff change to "Britannia" at Ilfracombe and leave at 5.30 p.m., arriving at Cardiff at 8.10 p.m.

Single Fare for the Steamer 15/- (Tickets on Board)

Return Fares to	ILFRACOMBE,	CARDIFF,	BRISTOL	OUT BY BOAT HOME BY RAIL
From **BRIGHTON**	40/-	35/-	30/-	Passengers from Worthing, Eastbourne and Hastings join the Steamer at Brighton (Palace Pier)
,, **WORTHING**	40/-	36/6	31/-	
,, **EASTBOURNE**	49/6	42/-	37/-	
,, **HASTINGS**	51/6	44/6	40/-	

The journeys from Bristol and Cardiff to Brighton may be made either via London or Salisbury. From Ilfracombe by the Salisbury and Southern Co. route only. Those to Eastbourne and Hastings via London only. Those to Worthing via the Salisbury and Southern Co. route only.

Tickets may be obtained in advance from Messrs. T. Cook & Son, 81, King's Road, Brighton, or at the Southern Railway Company's Booking Offices, Brighton, Worthing, Eastbourne and Hastings, available to return by any train carrying third-class passengers, up to and including Saturday, October 11th by the routes specified above.

Full particulars from Agents of P. & A. CAMPBELL Ltd.

W. REID, 53, Old Steine, Brighton.   Telegrams : "Ravenswood, Brighton."   Telephone : 5478 Brighton
W. A. PELLY, Pier, Eastbourne.   Telegrams : "Pier, Eastbourne."   Telephone : 1690 Eastbourne
A. J. McNAIR, Pier, Hastings.   Telegrams : "Pier, Hastings."   Telephone : 1032 Hastings

The Southern Publishing Co., Ltd., 130, North Street, Brighton—W1541

The timetable for the DEVONIA'S return trip to Bristol in 1930, destined to become one of the most stormy of all her round trips.

The WAVERLEY arriving at Shanklin in 1931. (CCC)

Capt. E. R. Smith on the bridge of the BRIGHTON BELLE. (ERK)

P. and A. CAMPBELL LIMITED

1931 SAILINGS FROM SWANSEA & MUMBLES 1931

White Funnel Fleet

(Weather and Circumstances permitting)

BY THE MAGNIFICENT NEW SALOON STEAMERS,

LADY MOYRA,

CAMBRIA, Etc.

SATURDAY, JULY 4th

LONG DAY TRIP TO ILFRACOMBE (allowing about 10 hours ashore)
Leave Swansea 9 a.m., returning from Ilfracombe 9 p.m. Fare 6/-
MORNING CRUISE TO ILFRACOMBE AND BACK
Leave Swansea 9 a.m., back about 1 p.m. Fare 5/-
LONG AFTERNOON TRIP TO ILFRACOMBE AND LUNDY ISLAND
Leave Swansea 2.10 p.m., Mumbles 2.25 p.m., returning from Lundy 7.30 p.m., Ilfracombe 9 p.m.
Special Return Fares—Ilfracombe 4/-, Lundy Island 5/6 (including landing and embarking at Lundy).
Passengers have about 5 hours in Ilfracombe, or about 2 hours on Lundy.
Passengers for Lundy will see the Greek Steamer "TAXIARCHIS"—wrecked on the Island and Salvage operations in progress.
Special S.W.T. Buses will leave Cambrian Place for all the outside districts advertised at the foot of this Bill, after the arrival of the "Lady Moyra" from Ilfracombe about 11 p.m.
NOTE—Steamer leaves Ilfracombe 11 a.m. for Swansea, and 9 p.m. for Mumbles and Swansea.

SUNDAY, JULY 5th

H.M. Battleship "MALAYA" will be at anchor off Weston and the "Lady Moyra" will sail around her
LONG DAY TRIP TO PORTHCAWL, MINEHEAD AND WESTON
Leave Swansea 9.45 a.m., returning from Weston 7.20 p.m., Porthcawl 10.15 p.m., back about 11.15 p.m.
Return Fares—Porthcawl 2/6, Minehead 4/-, Weston 5/6.
NOTE—This trip allows about 10½ hours in Porthcawl, 9 hours in Minehead or about 5½ hours in Weston.
Special S.W.T. Buses will be run this day to connect with the Lady Moyra for Porthcawl Minehead and Weston as follows :—
    Leave Ystradgynlais 8.15 a.m., Ystalyfera 8.23, Pontardawe 8.50, Clydach (Mond) 9.0, Morriston Cross 9.10, and arrive at South Dock Entrance 9.30 a.m.
    Leave Llanelly (Town Hall) 8.25 a.m., Loughor (Cross Keys) 8.55, Gorseinon 9.0, Fforestfach 9.15, and arrive at South Dock Entrance 9.30 a.m.
    Leave Briton Ferry (Villiers Street) 8.30 a.m., Neath (Victoria Gardens) 8.45, Skewen (Travellers Well) 8.55, Llansamlet 9.5, Bonymaen (Jersey Arms) 9.15, and arrive South Dock Entrance 9.30 a.m.
    Leave Gowerton 8.55 a.m., Dunvant Station 9.5, Killay (Siloam) 9.10, and arrive South Dock 9.30 a.m
    Leave Llangyfelach (Plough and Harrow) 9.5 a.m., Mynyddbach (Caersalem) 9.10, Treboeth Public Hall 9.15, and arrive South Dock Entrance 9.30 a.m.
Special S.W.T. Buses will return to all the Districts advertised above after the arrival of the Steamer about 11.15 p.m.
A Special Tram will leave Sketty at 9.10 a.m., and return from Mount Street after the Steamer arrives from Weston Minehead and Porthcawl about 11.15 p.m.

MONDAY, JULY 6th

DAY TRIP TO ILFRACOMBE (allowing about 6¾ hours ashore)
Leave Swansea 8.45 a.m., Mumbles 9 a.m., returning from Ilfracombe 5.30 p.m. Fare 6/-
CHEAP EVENING CRUISE ALONG THE GOWER COAST
Leave Mumbles Pier 7 p.m., Swansea 7.50 p.m. Back about 9.30. Fare 1/-. Children under 14 Half-price.

TUESDAY, JULY 7th

CHEAP DAY TRIP TO ILFRACOMBE, LYNMOUTH, MINEHEAD AND WESTON, passing the Battleship "MALAYA" at anchor off Weston.
Leave Swansea 8.45 a.m., Mumbles 9 a.m., returning from Weston 4.30 p.m., Minehead 6-15 p.m., Lynmouth 7 p.m., Ilfracombe 8-15 p.m.
NOTE—This Trip allows about 9½ hours at Ilfracombe, 8 hours at Lynmouth, 5½ hours at Minehead, or about 2½ hours at Weston.
Special Fares—Ilfracombe 5/-, Lynmouth 5/6, Minehead 6/-, Weston 6/6

WEDNESDAY, JULY 8th

LONG DAY TRIP TO LYNMOUTH, ILFRACOMBE, TENBY and a Cruise from Tenby.
Leave Swansea 8.45 a.m., Mumbles 9 a.m., returning from Tenby 4.30 p.m., Ilfracombe 7-15 p.m., Lynmouth 7-45 p.m. to Mumbles and Swansea.
This Trip allows 9 hours at Lynmouth, about 8 hours at Ilfracombe, or about 2½ hours at Tenby.
Return Fares—Lynmouth 6/-, Ilfracombe 6/-, Tenby 7/6, including Cruise 8/-

THURSDAY, JULY 9th

LONG DAY TRIP TO ILFRACOMBE (about 9 hours ashore)
Leave Swansea 9.15 a.m., Mumbles 9.30 a.m., returning from Ilfracombe 8-15 p.m. Fare 6/-
MORNING CRUISE TO ILFRACOMBE AND BACK
Leave Swansea 9.15 a.m., Mumbles 9.30 a.m., back about 1-30 p.m. Fare 5/-
LONG AFTERNOON TRIP TO ILFRACOMBE, and a Cruise from Ilfracombe.
Leave Swansea 2.45 p.m., Mumbles 3 p.m., returning from Ilfracombe 8.15 p.m. Fare 4/-, including Cruise 5/-
NOTE—This Trip allows about 3½ hours ashore.
Steamer leaves Ilfracombe 11.30 a.m. and 8.15 p.m. for Mumbles and Swansea
AFTERNOON CRUISE ALONG THE GOWER COAST
Leave Mumbles Pier 5 p.m. Fare 1/6, Children under 14 Half-price.
SINGLE TRIP TO BARRY, PENARTH, CARDIFF, CLEVEDON AND BRISTOL.
Leave Mumbles Pier 7 p.m. Fares—Barry Penarth or Cardiff 4/6, Clevedon or Bristol 6/-
NOTE—Steamer leaves Bristol 12 noon, Clevedon 1-10, Cardiff 2-15, Penarth 2-25, Barry 3 p.m. for Mumbles and Cruise

FRIDAY, JULY 10th

NO SAILINGS THIS DAY.

SATURDAY, JULY 11th

LONG DAY TRIP TO ILFRACOMBE (about 9 hours ashore)
Leave Swansea 9.15 a.m., Mumbles 9.30 a.m., returning from Ilfracombe 8.15 p.m. Fare 6/-
MORNING CRUISE TO ILFRACOMBE AND BACK.
Leave Swansea 9.15 a.m., Mumbles 9.30 a.m., back about 1-30 p.m. Fare 5/-
LONG AFTERNOON TRIP TO ILFRACOMBE (about 3½ hours ashore)
Leave Swansea 2.45 p.m., Mumbles 3 p.m., returning from Ilfracombe 8-15 p.m. Fare 4/-
NOTE—Steamer leaves Ilfracombe 11.30 a.m. and 8-15 p.m. for Mumbles and Swansea.

SUNDAY, JULY 12th

SPECIAL EXCURSION BY THE P.S. "LADY MOYRA."
Long Day Trip to Ilfracombe and Padstow (in Cornwall),
Leave Swansea 8-15 a.m., Mumbles 8-30 a.m., returning from Padstow 4-45 p.m., Ilfracombe 9 p.m.
NOTE—This Trip allows about 10½ hours at Ilfracombe, or about 3 hours in Padstow.
Return Fares—Ilfracombe 6/-, Padstow 10/-
MORNING TRIP TO ILFRACOMBE BY THE "LADY MOYRA," AND BACK (BY THE P.S. GLEN GOWER) (about 1 hour ashore)
Leave Swansea 8-15 a.m., Mumbles 8-30 a.m., returning from Ilfracombe 11-15 a.m., back about 1-15 p.m. Fare 5/-
Special S.W.T. Buses will be run this day to connect with the Lady Moyra for Ilfracombe and Padstow as follows—
    Leave Ystradgynlais 6.50 a.m., Ystalyfera 6.58, Pontardawe 7.25, Clydach (Mond) 7.35, Morriston Cross 7.45, and arrive at South Dock Entrance 8.5 a.m.
    Leave Llanelly (Town Hall) 7.0 a.m., Loughor (Cross Keys) 7.30, Gorseinon, 7.35, Fforestfach 7.50, and arrive at South Dock Entrance 8.5 a.m.
    Leave Briton Ferry (Villiers Street) 7.5 a.m., Neath (Victoria Gardens) 7.20, Skewen (Travellers Well) 7.35, Llansamlet 7.40, Bonymaen (Jersey Arms) 7.50, and arrive South Dock Entrance 8.5 a.m.
    Leave Gowerton 7.30 a.m., Dunvant Station 7.40, Killay (Siloam) 7.45, and arrive South Dock 8.5 a.m.
    Leave Llangyfelach (Plough & Harrow) 7.40 a.m., Mynyddbach (Caersalem) 7.45, Treboeth Public Hall 7.50, and arrive South Dock Entrance 8.5 a.m.
Special S.W.T. Buses will return to all the Districts advertised above after the arrival of the Steamer about 11 p.m. A Special Tram will leave Sketty 7.40 a.m., and return from Mount Street after the Steamer arrives from Padstow and Ilfracombe about 11 p.m.
AFTERNOON TRIP TO PORTHCAWL AND A CRUISE FROM PORTHCAWL UP CHANNEL
Leave Mumbles 12.45 p.m., Swansea 2-40 p.m., returning from Porthcawl 5.20 p.m. Fare 2/-, including cruise 3/-
Passengers landing at Porthcawl have about 1¾ hours ashore.
EVENING TRIP TO ILFRACOMBE by the "Glen Gower," and back by the "Lady Moyra."
Leave Swansea 6-30 p.m., Mumbles 6-45 p.m., returning from Ilfracombe 9 p.m. Fare 3/6
NOTE—Steamer leaves Ilfracombe 11-15 a.m. and 9 p.m. for Mumbles and Swansea.
The Ordinary Services of the S.W.T. Buses will connect with the P.S. "Glen Gower" for Ilfracombe at 6-30 p.m. and Special Buses will return to all the Districts advertised above after the arrival of the "Lady Moyra" at 11 p.m.

The Bristol Channel & District Guide. 1930.

P. & A. CAMPBELL Ltd

WINE LIST.

WINES & SPIRITS

	Per Glass		Per Glass
Whisky and Syphon Soda	10d.	Fine Old Cognac Brandy	1/-
Fine Old Highland Malt,		Martell or Hennessy***	1/3
John Walker, Scotch		Martineau, 20 years old	1/6
Whisky, Black & White,		Fine Jamaica Rum	9d.
Dewar's, and other Pro-		Best London Gin	9d.
prietary Brands	9d.	De Kuyper's Hollands	9d.
Old Dublin Malt Whisky...	9d.	Port or Sherry	8d.

LIQUEURS, CORDIALS and APERITIFS.

	Per Glass		Per Glass
Benedictine	1/-	Gin and Vermouth	9d.
Creme de Menthe	1/-	Apollinaris (Baby Polly)	4d.
Chartreuse (Yellow)	1/6	Schweppe's Mineral Waters	6d.
Peppermint	6d.	(Baby)	4d.
Liqueur Ginger Brandy	1/-	Other" Minerals	4d.
Kummel	1/-	Baby Soda	3d.
Gin and Orange	9d.		

WHITE WINES.

	Bot.	½-Bot.
Sauternes, Old	6/-	3/6
Chablis	6/-	3/6
Liebfraumilch	7/6	4/-

RED WINES.

	Bot.	½-Bot.
Burgundy, Beaune	5/-	3/-
Claret, Medoc	4/-	2/6
,, St. Julien...	5/-	3/-

SPARKLING WINES.

	Bot.	½-Bot.
Heidseick, Dry Monopole	20/-	10/6
Polnud, Ex. Quality, Ex. Dry	12/6	6/6
Golden Guinea, Dry	13/6	7/-

FINEST HAVANA CIGARS.

ALES, &c.

	½-Bot.		½-Bot.
Bass's Pale Ale	8d.	Lager Beer	8d.
Guinness's Extra Stout	8d.	Home Brewed	6d.
Champagne Cyder	6d.		

P. & A. CAMPBELL Ltd

TARIFF.

	s.	d.
BREAKFAST—Plain, with Bread and Butter, Marmalade, etc.	1	6
With Porridge, Fish, etc., etc.	2	0
With Porridge, Ham and Egg	2	6
With Porridge, Fish, Ham and Egg, etc.	3	0
COLD LUNCHEON—With Cold Meat, Salad, Sweets or Cheese	2	6
With Soup, Cold Salmon, Cold Meat, Salad, Sweets or Cheese	3	0
HOT LUNCHEON—With Soup, Fish, Joint, Vegetables, (See Menu) Sweets, Cheese	3	6
SPECIAL LATE DINNERS—Passengers desiring dinner on homeward journey are requested to order on outward journey.		
TEA—Plain, with Preserves, Cake, Bread and Butter	1	6
With Fried Fillets Plaice (or other Fish), etc.	2	0
With Cold Meat, Salad, etc., etc.	2	0
With Cold Salmon, etc., etc.	2	6
With Fried Fish, Cold Meat, Salad, etc.	2	6
With Salmon, Cold Meat, Salad, etc., etc.	3	0
Stewed Fruit or other Cold Sweets served with above ... extra		6

Special requirements will be catered for if notice is given on outward journey.

SUNDRIES.

Served in Lounge.

Cup of Tea, Coffee, or Cocoa		3d.
Ditto, with Bread and Butter or Biscuits		6d.
Small Cakes		2d.
Cake	per slice	3d.
Sandwiches	each	4d.
Biscuits and Cheese		6d.
Bovril or Oxo	per cup	4d.
Lemon or Orange Crush		3d.
Ices	per glass	4d.
Horlick's Malted Milk		4d. & 6d.

CHOCOLATES CAN BE OBTAINED ON BOARD

Any complaints as to incivility or overcharge should be made to the Chief Steward at once, or address to: Superintendent, Catering Department, P. & A. Campbell Ltd., Cumberland Basin, Bristol.

For Wines and Spirits List, see following page.

Tariff & Wine List. 1930.

The GLEN AVON takes a full complement of passengers from Cardiff to Weston in the 1930's. (ERK)

The BRITANNIA leaves Birnbeck Pier, Weston, having berthed, somewhat unusually, "bow out". (CCC)

A peaceful Sunday in the Floating Harbour, Bristol, in the early 1930's. Two boatmen drift past the DEVONIA while, in the distance, a tug rests at her berth, and the spires of Bristol Cathedral survey the tranquil scene. (ERK)

Aboard the RAVENSWOOD in the 1930's. (ERK)

Chapter 6 – 1932/1933

SOUTH DEVON.

In order to put the new venture into perspective we must go back beyond 1932 to look, briefly, at the history of excursion steamers in South Devon.

Over the years there were many small vessels which ran short, local cruises from a variety of resorts, harbours and estuaries, but the steamer services of the type dealt with in this narrative began in 1888, when a vessel named the **PRINCE,** of 61 gross tons and length of 128ft., was purchased by the partners Ellet and Matthews, of Exmouth, for services mainly from Torquay.

Her owners are credited with the invention of the apparatus required to land passengers on the, sometimes, steeply shelving beaches on that part of the coast. Landing was accomplished by dropping the stern anchor as the ship approached the shore, and when the specially strengthened bow had grounded on the sand or shingle, the stern anchor rope was hauled tight enough to hold the vessel bow on to the shore. In "South Coast Pleasure Steamers", Mr.Thornton states:-

> "A landing platform was then lifted over the side of the bow by a block and
> tackle on board and the passengers went ashore via this long and springy
> contraption, on which all right-minded children delighted to jump, eliciting and
> enjoying the shrieks of the Victorian and, later, Edwardian ladies. It seems to
> have been a somewhat hazardous business and had to be abandoned in anything
> like a swell."

In fact, it was the downfall of one steamer. Furthermore, it was not uncommon for the weather to deteriorate during the day, rendering it impossible for the steamer to call at the beach on the homeward journey. Consequently, the stranded passengers were then left to return to their destinations by their own devices. Despite the hazards, such trips became extremely popular, not least because of their novelty value.

The success of Ellet & Matthews first few seasons led to the formation of the Devon Steamship Co., taking delivery, in 1891, of their new steamer, the **DUCHESS OF DEVONSHIRE.** She had been built by R. & H. Green, of Blackwall and, with her gross tonnage of 221 and length of 170ft., replaced the **PRINCE.**

The **DUCHESS** became a most popular steamer and in 1896 she was joined by a slightly larger consort, also from the yard of R. & H. Green. The **DUKE OF DEVONSHIRE,** 257 gross tons and 175ft. long, was destined to sail the waters of the English Channel and beyond for many years. Both ships were transferred, in 1898, to the new Devon Dock, Pier & Steamship Co. Ltd. when the former concern went into liquidation.

Meanwhile, at Plymouth in 1895, the Plymouth Belle Steamship Co. Ltd. was formed, under the management of William Dusting, of Saltash. The company took delivery of a fine new paddle steamer, the **PLYMOUTH BELLE,** from Scott & Co., of Kinghorn, Firth of Forth. With her gross tonnage of 654 and length of 220ft., she possessed a full length promenade deck, an innovation on that part of the south coast at the time.

Her maiden trip was a cruise around the Eddystone lighthouse on Tuesday 9th. July 1895, and for most of the season she was engaged on three-day, weekend excursions from Penzance to Falmouth, Plymouth, Dartmouth and Torquay to Jersey and Guernsey. Her weekday trips alternated between lengthy coastal cruises and two-day journeys from Plymouth to Penzance and the Isles of Scilly. Plymouth, being primarily a naval and commercial base and a relatively minor resort, did not attract holidaymakers in sufficient numbers to support such an undertaking, and her first season was not a success. She spent the next three summers on charter, running from Eastbourne and Hastings, before being sold to German owners in 1899.

The **DUKE** and **DUCHESS,** however, continued to maintain their well patronised sailings until 1914. During the First World War the little **DUKE** distinguished herself by travelling as far afield as the Mediterranean Sea, where she was engaged on minesweeping duties in the Dardanelles. The **DUCHESS,** however, remained in home waters and, as we have seen, was on charter to P. & A. Campbell Ltd. to maintain the Cardiff to Weston ferry in the 1917 and 1918 seasons and to begin, and later supplement, the services of the returning White Funnel steamers during the 1919 season.

Both vessels returned to their South Devon duties in 1920 and remained unchallenged until 1925 when Cosens & Co., of Weymouth, ran their paddle steamer, **ALEXANDRA,** from Torquay. It appears that this competition was "bought off" by the DDP & SS Co. after her 1927 season by their paying an annual subsidy to her owners.

Further competition, although to a much lesser degree, was encountered from the Great Western Railway's tenders at Plymouth, which ran coastal cruises and trips to Torquay, often combined with a return trip by train. However, these vessels became more and more involved with their tendering duties as the liner and mail trade at Plymouth reached a peak during the early 1930's.

The West Country did not escape the escalating effects of the depression and trade fell to such a degree that the **DUCHESS** was laid up at the end of the 1930 season, leaving the **DUKE** to maintain the DDP & SS Co. services alone in 1931 and 1932.

Such then is the background to P. & A. Campbell's venture to South Devon. Capt. Dan Taylor, with his customary thoroughness, had organised a varied programme of sailings to and from some of the most popular resorts from Dorset to Cornwall. The steamer chosen for the service was the **WESTWARD HO**, a most versatile ship and one far superior to any other vessel plying on that part of the coast at the time. She was fast enough to cope with the longer trips planned for her and manoeuvrable enough to enter some of the more restricted waterways and harbours.

She was to be based at Plymouth, where she berthed at the GWR's, Princess Royal Pontoon in Millbay Docks, and at Torquay, where she used the Princess Pier. The co-operation between Campbells and the GWR, instituted by Capt. Taylor, was excellent; passengers could book their tickets at the railway's office on Millbay Pier and they made available circular tickets, whereby passengers were able to travel one way by steamer and the other by train. This facility was particularly welcome in view of the steamer frequently running single trips between Plymouth and Torquay in order to vary her schedule by changing her port of departure on the following day. The circular trips would, hopefully, be patronised sufficiently to defray the cost of, what would otherwise be, unprofitable light running.

The **WESTWARD HO,** under the command of Capt. Bernard Hawken, entered service at Whitsun and ran from Swansea for nearly a week before being replaced by the **GLEN USK** and returning to Bristol to lay up temporarily. She was back in service on Monday 20th. June 1932 when she left Bristol at 18.55 for the direct run to Plymouth, arriving at 10.34 next day. Her first sailing took place on Wednesday 22nd. June, from Plymouth, at 14.30, when she took 98 passengers for a cruise to off Prawle Point. She returned to Plymouth for an evening cruise, at 19.00, to off Fowey with 226 passengers, returning at 21.30. The **DUKE OF DEVONSHIRE,** based at Torquay, continued her short trips and landed passengers at the beaches, something that the **WESTWARD HO** was not equipped to do. The White Funnel steamer sailed on Sundays, which the **DUKE** did not, and with her greater turn of speed, travelled much farther afield.

Her regular trips between Plymouth and Torquay were supplemented, during the 1932 season, by sailings to Fowey; Falmouth, with cruises to the Manacles Rocks and to off Black Head; Penzance, usually with a cruise to off Land's End or in Mount's Bay; Dartmouth and, occasionally, Weymouth. Her coastal cruises often took her past those resorts and beaches at which the **DUKE** called, such as Teignmouth, Exmouth, Brixham, Slapton Sands, Seaton and Lyme Regis.

A lucrative source of revenue was Plymouth Navy Week, which encompassed Bank Holiday Monday 1st. August. She ran three cruises up the Hamoaze of the River Tamar to land at Devonport Dockyard, allowing her passengers four hours ashore to view the warships and a variety of displays presented by the Royal Navy. Later that month, the Torbay Regatta kept her busy with cruises to follow the yacht racing.

She was not scheduled to call at Looe during the season but did so on Saturday 17th. September, at the request of the GWR. One of their tenders was scheduled to take an afternoon trip from Plymouth to Looe with an extending cruise but, owing to the demands of the liner traffic that day, she was unable to do so. P. & A. Campbell were asked if the **WESTWARD HO** would take their passengers, a request which the company was only too pleased to carry out. She sailed from Plymouth at 14.45 with 312 passengers but did not proceed beyond Looe because of dense fog.

Her season finished at the end of September and she was advertised to return from Plymouth to Falmouth, Ilfracombe and Bristol at 13.00 on Friday 30th. but owing to bad weather the trip was postponed. She left on the following morning at 08.00 and sailed direct to Bristol, with eight passengers.

The question of the success of her season was to be carefully considered during the forthcoming winter.

THE SUSSEX COAST STEAMERS.

The **WAVERLEY,** with Capt. Bruford in command, opened the Sussex Coast sailings at the beginning of May 1932. On Thursday 19th. May, while returning from Sandown and Shanklin to Brighton, one of her passengers was taken ill. After exchanging wireless messages she berthed alongside the warship, **HMS CONCORD,** whose doctor boarded her, but unfortunately the passenger died before medical assistance could be rendered.

For the first time in her White Funnel career, the **BRIGHTON BELLE** ran in the Bristol Channel. She entered service on Friday 13th. May for about a week and sailed mainly from Newport, under the command of her South Coast master, Capt. E. R. Smith, who was necessarily accompanied by a pilot - Capt. J. A. Harris fulfilling the role for the period.

The **DEVONIA** was the next steamer to sail south, on Wednesday 22nd. June, and was eventually joined by the **BRIGHTON BELLE** at the beginning of July.

The latter had re-entered service on Saturday 18th. June with Capt. W. F. Watson acting as pilot to Capt. Smith. She left Cardiff for Newhaven at 17.15 on Thursday 30th. June and rounded Bull Point at 20.45 where she met the full force of a SW gale. At a speed of six knots she pitched and laboured heavily until 22.10 when she turned back and anchored east of Bull Point for shelter. At 04.00 next day she proceeded and, still labouring heavily, passed the Longships at 14.40 and Start Point at 21.50, when the sea began to moderate. Her journey south had been been one of some urgency owing to the presence of the Battleship, **MALAYA,** anchored off Eastbourne. The **BRIGHTON BELLE** arrived at Newhaven at 10.35 on Saturday 2nd. July and, almost immediately, began running a series of cruises around the warship which were to continue over the next few days.

Meanwhile, on Sunday 3rd. July, the **DEVONIA** sailed from Brighton, Eastbourne, Hastings and Folkestone to Margate, the first such trip by the White Funnel Fleet for many years, and ran another post-war "first" on Monday 8th. August when she took a good complement of passengers on the 5½ hour crossing from Brighton to Le Havre.

Not to be "out-done" by her larger sister, the **BRIGHTON BELLE** made the first post-war call at Littlehampton, on Thursday 25th. August followed, on Sunday 28th. August by a unique occasion; her only crossing, in peacetime, to France. She sailed from Hastings to Boulogne where she was joined, a little while later, by the **DEVONIA,** from Brighton.

Yet another revival from the pre-war years took place on the following Sunday, 4th. September, when the **DEVONIA** ran a day trip to Cherbourg, leaving the French port on her return at 17.00 and arriving at Brighton at 23.30.

At the end of the season the **BRIGHTON BELLE** left Newhaven for Bristol on the night of Wednesday 21st. September and, next day was "chased" along the south coast by a heavy, following sea whipped up by an ESE gale

The **DEVONIA** arrived in Bristol on Wednesday 25th. September after experiencing a rough passage when she ran into the spell of bad weather which delayed the **WESTWARD HO'S** return from Plymouth, but, like the **BRIGHTON BELLE,** she arrived home safely.

The **WAVERLEY** was the most fortunate: her round trip passing uneventfully after closing the season on Sunday 2nd. October.

THE BRISTOL CHANNEL AND BEYOND.

The **GLEN USK**(Capt. Edward Calvert) and the **BRITANNIA**(Capt. Jack George) both entered service on Maundy Thursday 24th. March 1932. The latter, while returning from Ilfracombe to Bristol that evening, collided with the steamer, **CALCIUM,** outward bound at that most difficult part of the River Avon, the Horseshoe Bend. The **BRITANNIA** emerged unscathed but the **CALCIUM** received damage for which P. & A. Campbell Ltd. was later required to pay the sum of nearly £850.

The Bristol Channel season otherwise passed without mishap and without many notable events. The company was, however, fortunate enough to obtain a particularly welcome and profitable charter. The International Eucharistic Congress was held in Ireland and liners from all parts of the world, bringing representatives of the clergy and their followers, converged on Dublin. A fleet of tenders was required to take the passengers from their ships into the River Liffey and the **GLEN GOWER** was one of their number. She left Cardiff at 10.15 on Tuesday 21st. June carrying 15 passengers, and arrived in Dublin at 22.30 after a good passage. From the following day until Saturday 25th. June, under the command of Capt. J. A. Harris, she tendered the mv. **SATURNIA**, 23,940gt, of the Italian Cosulich Line, one of the largest motor ships of that time. The **GLEN GOWER** returned from Dublin at 06.00 on Sunday 26th. June to Barry and Avonmouth, where she arrived at 21.00, again after a good voyage.

The Royal Navy's courtesy visits to the Bristol Channel were now becoming regular events and 1932 was no exception. As usual, Gwyneth White gives the details:-

"We set out from Ilfracombe to Tenby on the Glen Usk, passing the cruiser, Exeter, lying about ½ mile off-shore. We headed straight for Worm's Head, at the western extremity of the Gower Coast, then across Carmarthen Bay, reaching Tenby in just under three hours. The aircraft carrier, Furious, was at anchor a couple of miles out with the Lady Moyra alongside, and after we had disembarked at the pier, the Glen Usk took out a big crowd of Tenby people to board her."

1932 – POSTSCRIPT

On the return journey of a day trip from Plymouth to Penzance on Thursday 11th. August, the **WESTWARD HO**, with about 240 passengers aboard, ran into dense fog off the South Devon coast. Her arrival time at Plymouth was 21.45 but at 23.30 she was forced to anchor in Plymouth Sound, on the breakwater side of Drake's Island. Capt. Dan Taylor and several other people were awaiting her arrival on the Millbay pier, and when he heard her clanging bell he remarked, "That's the Westward Ho. I know that bell too well to be mistaken." She eventually berthed at 01.30 on the following day. The newspapers reported the incident and included a number of interviews with the passengers. One of the most amusing was that given by Mr. Arthur Sprague, a retired GWR employee who stated that he had given an impromptu concert on a small 18-stringed harp which he had taken on the trip! He added, "I couldn't sing to them because I have no teeth. I played a few waltzes but everyone was too tired to dance." What a pity that Mr. Sprague's musical endeavours should have been so coolly received.

The question of Sunday sailings came to the fore again in August 1932. For many years most of the steamers called at most of the south coast resorts on Sundays, Bournemouth however, was the exception until 1928 when the Town Council relented. The **DEVONIA,** however, was the first steamer to call from Brighton on a Sunday when she arrived on the afternoon of 14th. August. From the tone of several newspaper articles and letters it appeared that the residents were expecting an invasion by hordes of rampaging hooligans but the reality could hardly have been different. The occasion reached the national press and the "Daily Mail" reported:-

"Since the Town Council lifted its veto of Sunday excursions, the Bournemouth residents have been wondering what type of folk the first Sunday steamer from Brighton would bring. The Chairman of the Piers Committee said, 'There is nothing at all to alarm the residents. A more orderly, quiet and respectable crowd could not have landed. Sweethearts, who had been holding each other closely aboard the Devonia, walked along the pier quite 12ins. apart.' "

1932 had produced fair summer weather and the loss of the previous year became a profit of £12,770. Nevertheless, the economic decline continued and in the winter of 1932/1933 nearly three million of the country's working population were unemployed. Unaware that history would show this to be its lowest point, the company considered that, despite the profit, stringent measures were required to ensure its survival. Various decisions were carried, one of which was that the directors agreed, with great reluctance, that the wages and salaries of all employees, except Mr. W. J. Banks, should be reduced by 5% from January 1st. 1933.   The South Devon venture had been looked at closely and had not been a success. Although cancellations had been few, the trips had been poorly patronised. However, the fact that such speculative operations often take time to become established, it was felt that the past season had not been a fair test. The company considered that the services were potentially viable and that a further trial was advisable which, with better weather and, hopefully, an improving financial climate, would produce a more accurate and conclusive result. Events then took a rather unexpected and surprising turn.

The company records state that between November 1932 and February 1933, several letters had been received from the Devon Dock, Pier & Steamship Co. Ltd., but do not elaborate as to their contents. The mystery is partially solved, however, by a Minute Book entry referring to the board meeting of Tuesday 21st. March 1933, which states:

"The Secretary read a further two letters from the DDP & SS Co. Ltd. and was instructed to repeat the offer of £1500 for the purchase of the steamer Duke of Devonshire, with the offer of an additional £175, this being half the amount of the yearly subsidy due, from her owners, to Cosens Ltd."

The competition between the **WESTWARD HO** and the **DUKE** had not been particularly intense but there was no doubt that each steamer had taken a certain amount of business from the other. The purchase price of £1500, offered by Campbell's for the Duke, was a very low figure indeed, and the half-yearly subsidy referred to was the cost of "buying off" Cosens competition, agreed in 1928. However, the DDP & SS Co. Ltd. wished to concentrate their efforts on other, more lucrative, branches of their business, which included the operation of the Starcross to Exmouth ferry, the running of their engineering works and the ownership of Exmouth Docks. Consequently, they wanted to withdraw from the coastal excursion trade and were prepared to accept any price for the **DUKE.**

On Tuesday 25th. April 1933 the Secretary reported that the DDP & SS Co. Ltd. had accepted Campbell's offer of £1675, the agreement was signed and sealed, Capt. Peter Campbell became managing owner and the **DUKE OF DEVONSHIRE** became a member of the White Funnel Fleet.

It appears strange, no doubt, that a company which, only about two years earlier, had been prepared to sell one of its own steamers, and which was now battling against the effects of a depressed economy, should buy a vessel which, although two years her junior, was no match for the far superior **WESTWARD HO** or any other member of the fleet. Obviously, the purchase price was much too tempting to resist and was well worth paying in order to keep her out of competition.

The matter, however, did not end there. The **DUCHESS OF DEVONSHIRE,** laid up since the end of the 1930 season, had also been placed on the market. One wonders if the undisclosed contents of the previous months' correspondence included any reference to the sale of the **DUCHESS** as well as the **DUKE;** even if it did, Campbell's were not prepared to take on a second vessel. The **DUCHESS** was, however, sold in the spring of 1933 to Capt. E. R. F. Colberd, a former director of the DDP & SS Co. Ltd., who ran the South Devon & West Bay SS Co. Ltd. of Lyme Regis. So, after all, the **WESTWARD HO** would still have a rival, and the stage was set for "Act Two" of the South Devon drama which was to continue from the following June.

During the winter months various improvements had been made to the accommodation of the **LADY MOYRA,** many of which were of a relatively minor nature, such as the installation of illuminated signs indicating "Dining Saloon", "Bar" etc. This seemingly insignificant change took on a more important aspect when they appeared in both English and French. The **LADY MOYRA** was destined to change places with the **DEVONIA** on the South Coast, to take over the prestigious cross-channel services. On Monday 1st. March she had been re-named **BRIGHTON QUEEN,** perpetuating the name of her famous pre-war antecedent, and her paddle box emblem became a representation of the coat of arms of Brighton. While altering her name the company also transferred her port of registry to Bristol, from Barrow - a legacy of her Furness Railway days. At the same time the ports of registry of several other steamers were similarly changed - the **BRIGHTON BELLE,** from Newhaven; the **DEVONIA,** from Cardiff; the **GLEN GOWER,** from Swansea, and the **GLEN USK** and **GLEN AVON,** from Newport.

The **BRIGHTON QUEEN** and the **DEVONIA** left Bristol on the morning of Tuesday 23rd. May 1933 to enter, together, the Corporation Graving Dock at Avonmouth, for five days. The **DEVONIA,** commanded by Capt. Riddell, opened the Swansea season on Friday 2nd. June. The **BRIGHTON QUEEN** began sailing on the same day, having been taken south by Capt. Couves, arriving at Brighton for the first time at 11.38 on Wednesday 31st. May, after a time of 23 hours and 29 minutes for the 365 mile journey from Cardiff and Ilfracombe, giving an average speed of 15.4 knots.

The **BRIGHTON BELLE** arrived at Newhaven on the morning of Friday 2nd. June, and the **WESTWARD HO** arrived at Plymouth later the same day, both having sailed light from Bristol.

The **WESTWARD HO** began sailing on Whit Saturday 3rd. June, but where was the newly-acquired **DUKE OF DEVONSHIRE?** She was still laid up in Exmouth Docks, with, as yet, no pre-season preparation in progress.

Saturday 17th. June marked the beginning of "Bristol-Brighton Week", a publicity venture during which the city and the town, in various ways, extolled the virtues of each other as well as itself. In Bristol, for instance, the city centre was floodlight with the

GLEN GOWER forming a centre piece at Broad Quay, and the steamers ran late night cruises in the River Avon to view the Clifton Suspension Bridge illuminations.

So far, the season was progressing satisfactorily and trips were, on the whole, well patronised. The **BRITANNIA** experienced a problem on the morning of Sunday 18th. June. She had sailed light from Avonmouth to Bristol in order to leave at 05.15 on one of her marathon day trips to Padstow. On arriving at Hotwells her engineers reported that a crack had been discovered in her main steam pipe. However, she proceeded to Cardiff as scheduled where her 68 passengers were transferred to the **GLEN USK** which had been detailed to take over the trip, no doubt to the displeasure of her crew who had returned to Cardiff only a few hours earlier after a late night cruise to Ilfracombe. Miss White then takes up the story:-

"It was quite a nice morning with plentiful patches of blue sky and little wind, or so it seemed. We called at Barry and left at 07.50 with about 120 passengers aboard. Once outside, the wind was very strong and cold and we kept close inshore as far as Breaksea Point, then began to pull out and the fun started. People in the bows were ordered back just in time, for as the waves grew bigger they came sweeping over until the deck was awash. Speed was reduced to half so that we seemed to make no headway at all but pitched and rolled like a cork. However, we persevered until abreast of Nash Point where, the last traces of shelter being removed, the waves became positively mountainous. I've experienced some rough trips but have never seen such huge seas so far up channel. Hopes of Padstow faded into the background and in fact we didn't even reach Ilfracombe. I didn't think Capt. Calvert would risk one of those combers broadside on but he turned the ship very skillfully and the relief on the faces of many of the passengers was quite noticeable. We arrived back at Barry at 10.00.

The **BRITANNIA'S** steam pipe was repaired during the course of the day and she made her way, light, to Barry in order to take her scheduled return sailing to Bristol at 23.00.

The Padstow passengers were given the choice of a refund of their fares or replacement tickets for the next such sailing. The Whites took the latter option and set off once more aboard the **BRITANNIA** for the Cornish port on Tuesday 18th. July. This time all went well until the latter part of the return journey:-

"We drew alongside Minehead Pier, aboard the Britannia, at 22.45. The Glen Avon had brought over a number of passengers on an evening trip and left again at 21.00 but some of her passengers had preferred to wait for this later sailing, and they had cause to be glad that they did!

As we approached Barry, off the Breaksea Light Vessel, we suddenly ran into a blanket-like wall of fog and stopped dead. Then we crawled forward a few yards at a time while soundings were taken at the bows and the whistle was blown constantly. Suddenly a faint voice was heard hailing us to enquire if we were the Glen Avon. We made out that it was a pilot speaking and that the Glen Avon had run aground near Rhoose. We at once dropped anchor and stood by in case she needed assistance. The pilot came on board to confer with the captain, then cruised off into the fog. It was 23.45 when we dropped anchor and at 00.30 a rocket shot up in the west with a glare of light eerily diffused by the fog. It was the signal that the Glen Avon had floated off and a little while later we heard her distinctive, squeaky whistle passing us, but she missed us in spite of our clanging bell.

The fog grew so thick that from the stern of the boat the bridge was hardly visible and the only sound that broke the uncanny silence were the intervals of furious hammering on the bell on the foremast. Free tea, coffee and biscuits were available in the saloon and we were becoming resigned to the thought of spending the night on board though our position, according to the pilot, was only half a mile off the breakwater. At 01.45, two hours after dropping anchor, the pilot came alongside again and offered to conduct us into Barry and as the Glen Avon seemed to be in no danger, the captain agreed and very, very slowly we started once more. It was only when we were actually passing between the lights at the entrance to Barry harbour that they became visible. There was no Glen Avon at the pontoon when we drew alongside at 02.15, she was at anchor in the roads, and as it was out of the question for the Britannia to continue to Penarth and Cardiff, the special train which had been waiting for the Glen Avon's passengers was placed at our disposal. After raising three cheers for Capt. George and being photographed by the press we bundled into it and left the station at 02.30."

The **GLEN AVON'S** grounding was fully reported in the press next day:-

"Nearly 100 trippers spent a night on the Bristol Channel when the pleasure steamer Glen Avon ran aground in thick fog.

The fog, which descended suddenly at about 17.00, prevailed all along the channel coastline, and at the Gower Coast resorts bathers, who one moment were enjoying the sunshine, were the next enveloped in a dense mist which completely enshrouded the bays.

The Glen Avon was returning to Barry, Penarth and Cardiff after an evening cruise to Minehead and owing to the thickness of the fog she had to proceed very slowly.

At 21.50, when nearing the Glamorgan coast, between Rhoose and Aberthaw, the steamer ran on to the pebble beach and was stranded for over two hours.

The lifeboats at Mumbles, Weston and Barry were alerted but their services were not required.

Several residents of Rhoose had their attention drawn to the beach by cries from the steamer, and on reaching the shore, passengers asked that messages should be sent from the local post office to their homes stating that they were stranded but in no danger.

The local postmistress was in bed when the alarm was given, but was roused and she quickly communicated with the Barry police. The Glen Avon spent the night in Barry Roads and landed her passengers early this morning before proceeding to Cardiff."

The **GLEN AVON** entered the Channel Dry Dock, Cardiff, later in the day and was back in service on the following Saturday.

The **CAMBRIA** had a short season that year, of only just over six weeks, entering service on Saturday 5th. August. One week later she was backing out of Birnbeck Pier, Weston, at 16.00 when she ran on to a mud bank and remained aground for about three hours, before floating off undamaged.

With regard to Weston-Super-Mare, it was often stated that many of the steamer passengers who visited the Somerset resort for the day, ventured no further thanBirnbeck Island; all the amenities that they required being on hand. In addition to the cafe, restaurant and bar there was a full range of amusements for both adults and children including a bioscope(cinema), swimming pool, waterchute, switchback railway, maze and helter-skelter. There was also the inevitable seaside photographer, with his large, polished wooden box camera, who photographed the passengers as they disembarked and displayed the prints ready for purchase on their return. Changes took place, however, in 1933.

Weston's Grand Pier, opened in the summer of 1904, had been built nearer the town centre and railway station, in the broad, semi-circular sweep of Weston Bay. Its Pavilion housed a fine, Edwardian theatre which seated 2000 people and which provided entertainment from Shakespeare, opera and ballet to music hall and boxing! On January 13th. 1930 the Pavilion was destroyed by fire. It was rebuilt and re-opened in 1933 but housed a large funfair instead of a theatre. Many of the Birnbeck Island amusements were therefore transferred to the Grand Pier.

Campbell's South Devon season was being maintained by the **WESTWARD HO** alone. By the end of July nothing had been done to the **DUKE OF DEVONSHIRE** and it was virtually certain that the company had no intention of using her but had bought her simply to keep her out of the way. The **WESTWARD HO'S** enhanced programme of sailings, planned by Capt. Taylor before his retirement at the end of 1932, came into being during August and September, when her schedule began to include occasional calls at Mevagissey, Looe and Bournemouth.

The 1933 season drew to its close without further incident and the exceptionally fine summer had given a favourable result overall with a profit of £25,532, virtually double that of the previous year and the highest since 1928. Straight away the directors announced their intention, not only to reinstate the employees 5% reduction of wages and salaries, but also to pay the arrears in the form of a bonus. Furthermore, Capt. Peter decided to forego the additional remuneration of 5% of the company profits, over £15,000, which had hitherto been paid to him.

The depression, in general, had begun to ease, albeit very slowly, but the situation in South Wales remained grim and passenger figures from Swansea, Cardiff and Newport were still relatively poor.

The good summer had put a clearer perspective on the South Devon experiment and the results were far from satisfactory. The SD & West Bay SS Co. Ltd. had followed a pattern of sailings similar to that of the DDP & SS Co. Ltd. but had based the **DUCHESS** mainly at Lyme Regis. Whether this was done by arrangement with Campbell's or whether it was a tactful move on the part of Capt. Colberd is not known, however, she had presented even less of a threat to the White Funnel steamer than the **DUKE** had done in 1932.

An analysis of the **WESTWARD HO'S** passenger figures shows that the majority embarked at Torquay and amounted to 25187, more than double the number from Plymouth. Her capacity, on her No. 3 certificate, was about 830 but the average number of passengers carried per trip was a mere 215. Few people took advantage of the circular ticket arrangement with the GWR and many of the numerous single trips between Plymouth and Torquay were consequently made with the steamer virtually empty.

Mr. Banks told the directors that in view of the heavy losses incurred during the past two seasons on the Plymouth and Torquay services, he did not feel justified in recommending to the board to send the **WESTWARD HO** there during the following season.

Aboard the GLEN GOWER off Clovelly in the early 1930's. (HGO)

Whit-Monday 15th. May 1932. A still, hazy morning with hardly a ripple on the surface of the River Avon. The BRIGHTON BELLE leaves Bristol for Weston and Barry. (ERK)

The GLEN GOWER in Dublin Bay, June 1932. Behind her are some of the liners which brought delegates to Ireland for the International Eucharistic Congress. (CCC)

The first call at Littlehampton since 1914. The BRIGHTON BELLE arrives on Thursday 25th. August 1932. (HAA)

A unique occasion. The BRIGHTON BELLE at Boulogne on Sunday 28th. August 1932, her only peacetime visit to France. The DEVONIA passes on her arrival from Brighton. (CCC)

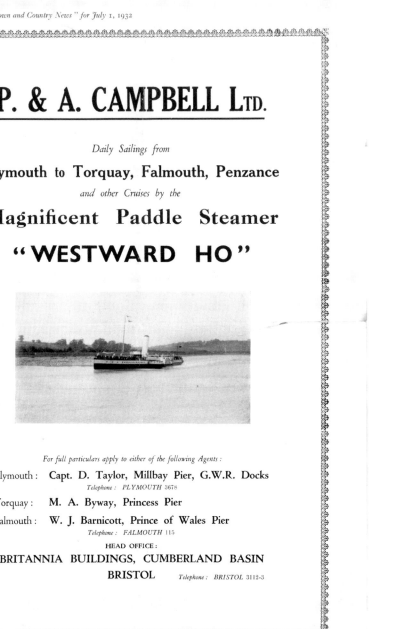

P. & A. CAMPBELL Ltd.

Daily Sailings from

Plymouth to Torquay, Falmouth, Penzance

and other Cruises by the

Magnificent Paddle Steamer

"WESTWARD HO"

For full particulars apply to either of the following Agents :

Plymouth : **Capt. D. Taylor, Millbay Pier, G.W.R. Docks**
Telephone : PLYMOUTH 3678

Torquay : **M. A. Byway, Princess Pier**

Falmouth : **W. J. Barnicott, Prince of Wales Pier**
Telephone : FALMOUTH 115

HEAD OFFICE :

BRITANNIA BUILDINGS, CUMBERLAND BASIN
BRISTOL   *Telephone : BRISTOL 3112-3*

This, and following two pages. Publicity leaflet for the WESTWARD HO's Plymouth venture. Unfortunately, the caption writer was mistaken, the steamer pictured is the CAMBRIA.

A VOYAGE IN THE BRISTOL CHANNEL

Westward Ho! in a Pleasure Steamer

By JOHN LANGDALE

In 1497 John Cabot sailed from Bristol and discovered Newfoundland. Ever since then, Bristol has been the gateway of adventure and romance for Englishmen.

P.S. *Westward Ho* lying in Cumberland Basin.

P.S. *Westward Ho.* Promenade deck after end.

Sea-venturers still sail from her quays. Their destination may not be so distant, their comforts greater, and their perils non-existent, but for the folk who crowd the decks it is none the less a great adventure.

Inlanders! Townsmen and countrymen, seeing the sea after a year of absence, perhaps even for the first time in their lives, yet greeting it as an old friend, because the love of the sea is in the English blood. No wonder they are

not satisfied to sit beside it, to paddle or to bathe. They must venture out upon its broad bosom and feel the fresh sea-breeze, unsheltered by the land.

That is why the pleasure-steamers of Messrs. P. and A. Campbell Ltd. are so crowded with happy holiday-makers every day throughout the summer when they sail from Hotwells, Bristol, in quest of adventure and exploration up and down the lovely Bristol Channel.

For lovely it is, a perfect cruising ground, with such variety that you can sail every day for a week and find new wonders to admire.

Sometimes, when the sky is cloudless and the Channel is a rich blue, you might fancy yourself in the Mediterranean or the Aegean. You look across at the mountains

The P.S. *Glen Usk* lying at Hotwells Landing Stage.

Wrong again! Apart from the GLEN USK photograph, all other illustrations show the BRITANNIA.

of South Wales, brown and shimmering in the heat, and it is easy to think them the legendary mountains of Greece.

Or again you may be hugging the coast of North Devon, and the sheer cliffs are more suggestive of Norway. Is there any coastal scenery to compare in colours with this stretch from Porlock to Ilfracombe ? Red cliffs, close green turf, patches of darker green, purple and gold ! Exmoor's sea of colour seems to spill over the lip of the moor and mingle with the splendours of rock and wave.

You come to Lynmouth round the great shoulder of Countisbury Hill where you may pick out the cars, crawling like insects, hugging the apparently sheer side of the cliff and painfully surmounting one of the stiffest gradients in England. The village itself is a cluster of

P.S. *Westward Ho* The Dining Saloon.

P.S. *Westward Ho.* The Lounge.

always had the reputation of being the smartest, most comfortable service operating in the Bristol Channel. Its saloon steamers are beautifully equipped and splendidly manned. Meals and refreshments are obtainable on board at the most reasonable prices, and the fares are low.

Visitors sometimes ask : " What happens to these men during the winter ? Are they thrown out of work ? " In this case, fortunately no. Messrs. Campbell have a works where they do their own repairs during the winter. They also manufacture the special Campbell and Banks' Patent Piston Ring, a device now fitted by almost all big shipping lines in the world, and the invention of a member of the firm.

white houses and hotels, wedged in a cleft of the wooded hills where the River Lyn breaks through to the sea. Here the boats put out as we cast anchor and we feel a little thrill as though we were really going ashore in some foreign port.

This is only one cruise you may take by this well-known line of steamers. Among the other places which can be visited are Clevedon, Cardiff, Penarth, Barry, Newport, Minehead and Ilfracombe. You may have a real adventure, sailing round from Bristol to Brighton and taking two days over it, while the shortest trips of all take only the afternoon or the evening. Full particulars can be had from Messrs. Campbell at Cumberland Basin, Bristol.

This famous line of pleasure-steamers dates from 1887 and has

P.S. *Westward Ho.* The Engine Room.

The WESTWARD HO arriving at Torquay. 1932. (CCC)

1932   **P. & A. CAMPBELL LTD.**   32
WHITE FUNNEL FLEET

SAILINGS from FALMOUTH

(Prince of Wales Pier)

(Weather and Circumstances
Permitting)

By the Saloon
Passenger Steamer

'Westward Ho'

GRAND DAY TRIP TO

Sunday, Sept. 4th	**PENZANCE**

(About 2½ hours ashore)

Leave 12.20 p.m.; return Penzance 5.0 p.m., back about 7.10 p.m.   **Fare 5/-.**

Passengers may, if they desire, stop on board at Penzance for the cruise to
LAND'S END by payment of 1/- extra.

SINGLE TRIP TO PLYMOUTH

Leave 7.20 p.m.   **Fare 4 -**   (Millbay Pier, G.W.R.)
Note:—Steamer leaves Plymouth 9.30 a.m. for Falmouth.

Tuesday, Sept. 6th

Afternoon Cruise along the Coast
passing the Manacles and towards Black Head

Leave 2.30 p.m., back about 4.15 p.m.   **Fare 1/6**

SINGLE TRIP TO FOWEY AND PLYMOUTH.   Leave 4.30 p.m.

Fares: Fowey 2/6; Plymouth 4 - Note: Steamer leaves Plymouth 9.30 a.m., Fowey 10.45 a.m. for Falmouth.

GRAND DAY TRIP TO

Friday, Sept. 9th	**PENZANCE**

(About **3** hours ashore).   Leave 11.45 a.m.; return Penzance 4.45 p.m.; back about 7.0 p.m.   **Fare 5/-.**

Passengers may, if they desire, stop on board at Penzance for the cruise to Land's End on payment of 1/- extra.

SINGLE TRIP TO PLYMOUTH

Leave 7.10 p.m.   **Fare 4/-.**   (Millbay Pier G.W.R.)
Note: Steamer Leaves Plymouth 9.0 a.m. for Falmouth.

SINGLE FARE TO PLYMOUTH **4/-.** TO PENZANCE **4/-.** TO FOWEY **2/6.**

TAKE TICKETS ON BOARD STEAMER. - THE ABOVE FARE INCLUDES PIER TOLLS AT PLYMOUTH.

Children under 14 Half-Fare. Dogs, Bicycles, Prams or Mail Carts (at owner's risk), **2 -** Single or Return. The Company cannot convey
Motor Cycles or Side Cars.

SPECIAL TERMS FOR PARTIES. BREAKFASTS, LUNCHEONS, TEAS, REFRESHMENTS, Etc., served on board at moderate terms.

The Company reserve the right to alter the advertised times or withdraw any of the above sailings as weather and other circumstances
may require. A reasonable quantity of Luggage (which must be labelled) carried Free of Charge at Passenger's risk.

SPECIAL NOTICE—Information regarding Sailings between Weston-s-Mare and Cardiff and Ilfracombe to all Bristol Channel Ports
can be obtained from W. J. Barnicoat, Prince of Wales Pier, Falmouth, or from the Company's Agents : D. Taylor, Millbay Pier ; G.W.R.
Docks), Plymouth ; R. H. Ward, Pier Gates, Weston-super-Mare ; F. W. Birmingham, 10 Quay, Ilfracombe ; or P. & A. Campbell, Ltd.,
Cumberland Basin, Bristol. Telephone Numbers : Plymouth 3638, Weston 44, Ilfracombe 156, Bristol 23112.

CORNISH ECHO CO., PRINTERS, CHURCH STREET, FALMOUTH.

The RAVENSWOOD in the Avon. Tuesday 17th. May, 1932. Aft of the sponson, between the horizontal gold lines on her black hull, can be seen the additional portholes which cast extra light into the dining saloon. A feature unique to the RAVENSWOOD. (ERK)

The BRIGHTON QUEEN in dry dock at Avonmouth. Wednesday 24th. May 1933. Ahead of her is the DEVONIA. (ERK)

On a Saturday afternoon in the fine summer of 1933, Capt. W. A. Couves brings the BRIGHTON QUEEN alongside the pier at Ryde, Isle of Wight. (CCC)

The GLEN AVON in the Avon. Sunday 4th. June, 1933. (ERK)

The GLEN GOWER about to swing on an ebb tide at Swansea. 1933. (HGO)

The DEVONIA turning at Pockett's Wharf, Swansea. 1933. (HGO)

The English Channel Guide, issued in 1933.

The WESTWARD HO at her berth in Millbay Dock, Plymouth, about to depart on an afternoon cruise to Devonport Dockyard. August 1933. (CCC)

The Torbay Regatta. The WESTWARD HO follows the progress of a racing yacht. (CCC)

Chapter 7 – 1934/1935

With the company's withdrawal from South Devon, the **DUKE OF DEVONSHIRE** was placed on the market. On Tuesday 20th. February 1934, Mr. Banks informed the board that, at a recent meeting with Capt. Colberd, he had suggested that the South Devon company might be willing to purchase her. While the matter was under consideration an offer of £1400 for the vessel was received from Jeremiah Dwyer of the Rocksavage Engineering Co. of Cork, subject to her obtaining a No.4 passenger certificate. She went on to the gridiron at Exmouth for inspection and, terms having been agreed, the Bill of Sale was signed and sealed on Tuesday 24th. April. The **DUKE** left Exmouth at 11.50 on Tuesday 1st. May for Ireland, and eventually arrived at Cork on the morning of Saturday 5th. May, having encountered some very rough weather on the way. She was to return to the South Coast two years later. Purchased by Cosens and re-named **CONSUL,** she remained in their ownership until the mid-1960's when she reverted to her original name on being sold for use as a sailing club headquarters, moored in the River Dart. She was finally broken up in 1968, after 72 years of service.

The **DUCHESS OF DEVONSHIRE,** now without the Campbell competition, resumed her sailings in 1934 from Torquay, but came to a sad end on Monday 27th. August when landing on the beach at Sidmouth. Her stern anchor rope, by which she would have been held bows on to the beach, parted and the sea washed her broadside on to the shingle, where she settled across a groyne and became so badly damaged that she was broken up where she lay.

P. & A. Campbell's improving financial situation meant that they were now able to embark on a programme of essential maintenance and refurbishment required by several members of the fleet.

The **BRIGHTON BELLE** left Bristol at 08.00 on Tuesday 6th. March bound for Barrow-in-Furness, where she was to be reboilered. Under the command of Capt. E. R. Smith she made a good passage and arrived at Barrow at about 14.30 next day. She arrived back in Bristol on Friday 20th. April, her appearance slightly altered. Her bridge had been moved forward and had been turned around, through 190°, so that the wings were now at the after end; the safety valve steam pipe was now forward of the funnel and she had been given a chime whistle.

Such whistles became a most distinctive feature of the Campbell steamers and most of them were so fitted during the winter of 1933/1934. The exceptions being the **BRITANNIA**, which had one from the time of her building, the **BRIGHTON QUEEN,** which was fitted with one before her first south coast season in the previous year, and the **CAMBRIA,** which never had one. The latter, however, was even more of an exception in this respect in that she possessed, as well as the conventional organ whistle, a siren, inherited from the **PRINCESS MAY,** the small steamer operated by Peter and Alec on their own account for a short period in 1902. A good friend of the writer, Mr. Sydney Robinson of Penarth, recalls with wry amusement:-

> "My word, the Cambria's siren was loud; it made people jump out of their shoes! Often, when approaching Hotwells landing stage in the silence of a late night, the siren was sounded to warn the pontoon men of her arrival. The blast

echoed around the high cliffs of the Avon Gorge for what seemed to be minutes."

Most of the steamers had been fitted originally with organ whistles, which gave a single note of a pitch which varied according to the size of the hollow brass tube into which steam was forced. The chime whistle was of greater diameter and inside was divided into several chambers, with the result that it gave a particularly harmonious note. Another friend of the writer, Mr. John Brown of Cheltenham, once explained that an accurate representation of it could be obtained on a church organ. Those of a musical inclination, with access to a keyboard, will find that the notes B flat, D and G, played in unison will give a reasonable idea of the once familiar sound.

A few days after returning from Barrow the **BRIGHTON BELLE** went into Hill's Dry Dock in company with the **WAVERLEY,** when the opportunity was taken to fit the latter with a bow rudder, steered by a wheel on the foredeck, which was of great assistance in turning the ship in narrow waterways.

From 1934 the Board of Trade were no longer prepared to allow the **WAVERLEY** to cross the English Channel to France, so much was required by way of alterations that the company deemed it too expensive. As the Boulogne traffic warranted the support of a second vessel a re-arrangement of steamers was necessary. The **GLEN GOWER** had been built with cross channel sailings in mind but even she did not fully conform to the the Board of Trade's requirements, which were then far more stringent than when she was built, twelve years before. They called for the fitting of an extra bulkhead, a radio direction finder and the replacement of her five lifeboats with those of larger dimensions and capacity. Once these alterations had been carried out she was to replace the **WAVERLEY** on the south coast and supplement the **BRIGHTON QUEEN'S** continental visits. Accordingly she left Cardiff for Newhaven, with Capt. Bruford in command, on Thursday 17th. May 1934.

The **WAVERLEY** opened the Swansea season on Friday 18th. May, but was relieved, a week later, by the **GLEN USK** until the **DEVONIA** arrived in mid-June. In the meantime, the **WAVERLEY** had been taken over by Capt. George at the end of May and spent the rest of the season running from Bristol in place of the **BRITANNIA.** The latter was out of service for the whole of that season, undergoing an extensive overhaul which was to include the refurbishment of her accommodation in the style of the period, the construction of a deckhouse over the after companionway and, subsequently, the installation of a new, haystack boiler.

The Whitsun weekend was very fine, hopefully the portent of a good summer! However, the **BRIGHTON QUEEN'S** round trip to Brighton began in anything but summer conditions. The intrepid Miss White made the journey:-

"Thursday 21st. and Friday 22nd. May 1934.

09.45 this morning found me on the pier, one of the two passengers from Penarth bound for Brighton. It was not a promising sort of morning and was making attempts at raining when the Brighton Queen rolled up, just a few minutes late, and the great trip began...... At 16.30 we backed out of Ilfracombe with 132 passengers aboard, many of whom had come from the South Coast by train via Bristol, Cardiff or Ilfracombe to make the trip around.

After passing Bull Point the wind freshened, which I hoped would dispel the thick drizzle which blotted out every trace of coastline. The further we went the windier it became until we were pitching and tossing, head right into the wind. Hartland Point could not be seen but we heared its distinctive foghorn with the puny little grunt at the end of each blast. It became so bad that speed was reduced to half and it was not at all an enjoyable portion of the trip. There were many "casualties", (ie. seasick), which, as most of the crowd were seasoned "round trippers", says much for the conditions. One of the funniest characters among the passengers was an old French woman from London, who for years has made the journey on every boat that goes around and back, that is six times per year. She is an amazing person who trots around the ship with perfect equilibrium while everyone else, including the crew, is staggering and flopping around in all directions! At 18.45 speed was further reduced to slow while the ropes and buoyant seats in the bow were removed and lashed down on the after deck.

We then continued at half speed and it was not until 21.30 that we had our first glimpse of land, Trevose Head, whose red light winked cheerfully after us for many miles. Then we saw little more until the Godrevy Light and the lights of St. Ives at about 00.30, on Friday morning when speed was, at last, increased to full again.

As there is no sleeping accommodation on the steamers you just have to curl up with a rug in the saloon or the ladies cabin, but none of these alternatives was very pleasant. The saloon was kicking about like a bucking broncho and both places looked like hospital wards; even the two stewardesses were ill! So I preferred to curl up in a chair in the most sheltered part of the deck, which I had the forethought to "bag" early, joining the handful of passengers who remained on deck all night. It may have been colder but I am certain that it was far pleasanter than down below. I had been on trips which rolled more but none that pitched and tossed like this one did, with the stern waving about in mid-air and the after lifeboat looking as though it was going to break loose from the davits....

After the great revolving light of Pendeen Watch came Land's End and the Longships. With the decks awash we had a terrific thumping and shaking as we turned the corner from the Bristol into the English Channel, but once around, with the south westerly wind behind her, the difference in the motion of the ship was considerable; it was much gentler with the huge seas following her as we began our crossing of Mount's Bay at about 01.30. I must have fallen asleep because I awoke to find the Lizard light revolving in my eyes, then I dropped off again until the dawn was breaking and we had just left the Eddystone astern. Feeling decidedly stiff and chilly, I went below for a wash and a hot drink then, with circulation restored, I went back on deck to enjoy the scenery until breakfast, which was nearly two hours off, it being only 05.30. We had kept well out from Plymouth but the coast of Bolt Head and Start Point were passed close inshore so that we could see up the estuaries of Salcombe and the Dart as well as the coastline towards Brixham. When the coast receded around Lyme Bay I went below for breakfast without missing much. I was extremely hungry and to judge by the crowd in the dining saloon, all of the "casualties" of the night had made a full recovery and were feeling ravenous!

The weather was improving and it became a beautiful day, with a fresh wind, racing clouds, blue sky and sea flecked with white horses. After crossing Lyme Bay we rounded Portland Bill at about 11.30, when several destroyers and a submarine were entering the harbour. After the Dorset coast we passed the Needles, Isle of Wight, at about lunchtime but the coastline after Portsmouth and Selsey Bill becomes flat and rather monotonous; one resort follows another, Bognor Regis, Littlehampton and Worthing, but behind the latter, the South Downs rise to give it interest. Worthing merges into Hove, and Hove into Brighton, beyond which the white cliffs of the Seven Sisters rise again towards Newhaven and Beachy Head. The Glen Gower was leaving in that direction as we drew into Palace Pier at 17.00, two hours overdue and 24½ hours out of Ilfracombe."

To illustrate the extreme contrasts experienced in sailing on the Campbell steamers, Miss White describes another trip, later that season:-

"Friday 29th. June 1934.

We had a pleasant evening trip up the River Usk, to Newport, leaving Penarth at about 18.30 in the Glen Usk, which had come up from Ilfracombe. We went into Cardiff where most of the crowd disembarked, just a fair number coming on for the cruise. From Cardiff, we turned eastward and followed the flat shore, the mountains behind hardly visible through the dense heat haze. Less than half an hour brought us to the mouth of the Usk, where speed was reduced for the winding, tortuous course of about four miles to the town bridge. It was an interesting run with the docks on the port side and, ahead, the beautiful transporter bridge assuming gigantic proportions. At Cashmore's ship breaking yard two destroyers and a submarine were in the process of demolition. Soon we entered the straight reach terminating at the bridge, with the landing stage alongside. The manoeuvring of the steamer to the pontoon, on a flood tide, is among the smartest examples of seamanship I know. The ship turns sharply to starboard and the bows are driven a few feet into the mud of the river bank several hundred yards downstream from the landing place. The flow of the tide swings her around, she then backs off and approaches the pontoon stern first. The Newport passengers disembarked and she was quickly under way on the return journey, the sun setting as we sailed under the delicate tracery of the transporter bridge once more. We passed the Cambria at the mouth of the river, returning from a cruise around the English & Welsh Grounds Lightvessel, on her first day in service, before beginning the run down channel as dusk set in."

The first half of the season was blessed with mainly fine weather. On the south coast Mr. Thornton was enjoying his sailings:-

"I remember a particularly delightful journey from London to Swanage. The first stage was on the **ROYAL EAGLE** from Tower Pier to Ramsgate, where a change was made on to the **BRIGHTON QUEEN** for Brighton. The purser of the **BRIGHTON QUEEN,** Mr. Sydney Partington, was most co-operative, as always, and sent a wireless message to the **GLEN GOWER'S** purser, Mr. Cyril Lyons, for a room to be booked for me in an hotel opposite the Palace Pier, owing to the lateness of the hour of arrival. Then, after a day ashore in Brighton, the journey was resumed, again aboard the **BRIGHTON QUEEN,** via Ryde and the Solent, to Bournemouth. The trip to Swanage was completed on Cosens **MONARCH,** which, it must be admitted, was rather an anti-climax after the **ROYAL EAGLE** and **BRIGHTON QUEEN**.

The weather deteriorated from about mid July, and for the rest of the season remained very unsettled. Additional problems arose when the **BRIGHTON BELLE** suffered a major breakdown.

At 09.00 on Saturday 15th. September, while leaving Newhaven harbour, her high pressure cylinder cracked after the Chief Engineer had forgotten to open the drain valves. She returned to her berth and her sailings were cancelled.

The company had always given priority to its Bristol Channel services but under the prevailing circumstances, with the reduction in trade from the South Wales ports, those services were more than adequately covered and it was considered more beneficial to give priority to the South Coast sailings. The **WESTWARD HO** was therefore taken out of service at Cardiff on Sunday 16th. September to prepare to replace the **BRIGHTON BELLE.** She sailed at midnight, direct for Newhaven, without passengers and passed Hartland Point at 04.30, but, in deteriorating weather, at 06.45, in Port Isaac Bay, she was forced to turn back and shelter off Clovelly. At 13.40, the weather having moderated, she set off again, reaching Newhaven at 13.35 on Tuesday 18th. September.

At 23.15 that night the **BRIGHTON BELLE** left Newhaven, in tow of the tug, **FOREMOST 22,** for the long haul to Bristol.She was abeam of St. Catherine's Point, Isle of Wight, at 08.00 next day but, a few hours later, in a strong SW wind and rough sea, with an unfavourable weather forecast, she proceeded to Portland harbour, where she anchored at 15.15. She sheltered there until the morning of Friday 21st. September, when, after a diver had cleared her fouled anchor, she proceeded at 11.35. She rounded Land's End at 07.00 on Saturday 22nd. and all went well until 22.30 that night when a further gale, this time from the NW, caused her to heave to off Lynmouth Foreland for three hours. At 05.00 on the Sunday morning she anchored in Barry Roads and continued later in the day, with the tug, **VOLUNTEER,** at her bow and the **FOREMOST 22** astern, berthing alongside the **BRITANNIA** at the Underfall Yard, Bristol, at 21.00, after a voyage taking 4 days, 21 hours and 55 minutes!

The **WESTWARD HO** took over the **BRIGHTON BELLE'S** sailings on Wednesday 19th. September, running between Eastbourne and Hastings. She visited Brighton on one day only, Sunday 23rd. September, when she ran several cruises from both the West Pier and Palace Pier, and her only visit to Worthing was made on Sunday 30th. September. This, like her South Devon venture, formed another unique chapter in her history, being the only peacetime occasion when she visited the Sussex coast, and ended when she left Newhaven at 07.10 on Monday 1st. October to return, light, to Bristol.

The season produced a profit of £14,104. The director, Mr. G. H. Boucher, had been voted company chairman in June 1934 and his report to the shareholders, during the

43rd. Ordinary General Meeting, held at the Grand Hotel, Bristol, was particularly comprehensive:-

"'The results of the year's trading are very disappointing to your board and the weather has been mainly responsible', said Mr. Boucher.

In the early part of the summer the company expected to have a very favourable season. Fine weather, however, so essential to their well being, did not continue through July and August, and in September it was positively boisterous.

'A fine week in the early part of August is worth four or five good weeks in May, June or September. But, during the August Bank Holiday we carried only about three-quarters of the number of passengers we carried during the similar period in 1933. The fact that Easter came early in the year, 1st. April, thus giving a much longer season did not help us in the least because of the poor conditions, and although we had one less boat - the Britannia was out of commission - we ran 1400 miles further in 1934 than we did in 1933. There was an 8% fall in our receipts and this explains the decrease in our net profit. This proves that, only if we have good weather in July, August and September, can we have good results. There had been further economies but their progress depended, in a large measure, upon there being satisfactory industrial conditions in South Wales, Cardiff being our biggest port. Although the situation in South Wales continued at a low ebb, it was just a little better than it had been'.

A shareholder then asked why the company did not now advertise their trips in the Cardiff newspapers. Mr. W. J. Banks replied that the business the company were doing did not warrant it.

Mr. Boucher then continued, 'We left Plymouth out of our calculations last year and it was a good job that we did. Experience has taught us that we cannot make money on that part of the coast. We hope to make a fair amount of money at the Naval Review in the forthcoming July and shall spare every boat we can for our Isle of Wight station. The question as to whether we are to have a profitable season this year depends, not upon the efforts of board, but upon the weather conditions.'"

The **BRITANNIA'S** extensive overhaul, the refurbishment of her accommodation and the building of her deckhouse had been completed earlier in the year but her scheduled re-boilering was delayed. Although offered a £500 premium, Barclay & Curle were unable to accept her, owing to pressure of work, until the early spring of 1935. The job was rendered all the more necessary when, shortly after Christmas 1934, the existing boiler was found to have developed a number of cracks. In mid-February 1935 she entered Hill's Dry Dock and after bottom painting left Bristol for Glasgow. The memorandum book gives the details of the events of the ensuing weeks:-

"Tuesday 5th. March. 1935.
18.45.   Dep. Cumberland Basin for Glasgow, (Capt. J.George), in tow of tug,
          Eastleigh.

Wednesday 6th. March.
06.00.   Off Helwick Lightvessel. Fresh wind. Moderate sea.
11.00.   Steamer, Brora, reported Britannia off St. Anne's Head.
18.00.   Abeam of Fishguard.
Thursday 7th. March.
15.00.   Via Portpatrick Radio:- Britannia off Maughold Head, Isle of Man, in fog.
           Will proceed when weather clearer.
20.00.   Mull of Galloway abeam. Weather improved. All well.
Friday 8th. March.
09.15.   Passed Cumbrae.
15.00.   Arrived at Glasgow - Elderslie Dockyard. All well.
Monday 11th. March.
           Boiler lifted out.
Tuesday 26th. March.
           New boiler in.
Thursday 4th. April.
           Telegram from Glasgow :- 'Had steam test on boiler,
           Everything satisfactory. Have been in touch with Capt. Peter, steamer
           sailing tomorrow.'
Friday 5th. April.
           Telegram from Gourock.
           14.26. 'Left Gourock for Blairmore. Everything working satisfactorily.'
           Via Portpatrick Radio:- Left Blairmore 14.40.
           Ailsa Craig abeam 17.45. Strong NNW wind.
Saturday 6th. April.
           Via Burnham Radio:- South Bishop abeam 09.15.
           14.40.   Passed Scarweather.
           16.20.   Passed Barry.
           17.20.   Passed Clevedon.
           18.45.   Arrived at Hotwells Landing Stage.
           20.30.   Into Cumberland Basin.

She entered service on Maundy Thursday 18th. April for the Easter weekend. The improvements to her accommodation were much admired by the public and her new, large, flat sided funnel enhanced her elegant lines and contributed greatly to her powerful appearance.

It was then the **CAMBRIA'S** turn for an extensive overhaul and she was out of service for the whole of the 1935 season, her place being taken, at Cardiff, by the **WAVERLEY.**

The **WESTWARD HO** was also undergoing refurbishment but, unlike her two sister ships, the work did not necessitate her being taken out of service but was spread over the winters of 1934/1935 and 1935/1936. The only external change apparent in 1935 was her new funnel; taller, narrower and with a deeper cowl. The funnel, incidentally, was originally intended as a replacement for the **BRITANNIA,** following her reboilering, but preference was given to the larger, more modern design for the flagship of the fleet.

The **BRIGHTON QUEEN,** after running from Swansea during Whitsun week, sailed south on Thursday 20th. June, and on the following weekend ran a two day trip to Trouville-Deauville. The local press announced the full details :-

> "Repeating, with improvements, one of their most attractive trips of recent years, Messrs. P. & A. Campbell are arranging a special trip by the Brighton Queen to Trouville-Deauville and Lisieux.
>
> It will be a two-day trip. The Brighton Queen leaves the Palace Pier, Brighton at 12.50 on Saturday 22nd. June and arrives at Trouville Pier at about 18.45 the same day. The steamer remains at Trouville until 16.00 on Sunday and reaches Brighton again at about 21.45 that evening.
>
> This arrangement permits of agreeable alternatives. Those who wish can pass the night at Trouville and stay there until the boat leaves next day. Trouville-Deauville, it need hardly be said, is one of the smartest and gayest of French watering places, with a distinctive atmosphere of aristocracy. As an alternative, on the Sunday morning, a motor coach tour to Honfleur will be available.
>
> For others, the particular appeal of this trip is that it gives plenty of time to visit the picturesque old Normandy town of Lisieux and see the famous shrine of the saint in whose honour Lisieux has become a famous place of pilgrimage. The experience is one that blends, in unique fashion, medieval charm and modern activity.
>
> The company will arrange an inclusive fare, to cover hotel accommodation and expenses from Brighton to Brighton. The whole trip can be done for a little over thirty shillings".

This most attractive trip went according to plan but was, inexplicably, very poorly patronised by only 122 passengers, and although the occasional day trips to Trouville-Deauville continued, the overnight stay was never repeated.

The highlight of the season was the Silver Jubilee Royal Naval Review held at Spithead. As well as the involvement of the three south coast steamers, the **BRITANNIA** was sent around for the occasion. This was her first visit to the Sussex coast and proved to be a most arduous week.

She began by leaving Bristol at 03.30 on Thursday 11th. July and sailing direct to Ilfracombe where she arrived at about 07.30. At 10.15 she left on a day trip to Clovelly and Lundy, landing her passengers on the island at 12.45. After their time ashore they were to return in the **GLEN USK** and **WAVERLEY** while the **BRITANNIA** sailed light from Lundy, at 13.20, bound for Newhaven. She made good time down the Cornish coast, despite a heavy NW swell, rounding Land's End at 18.30. She passed Start Point at 23.50 and moored in Newhaven at 09.05 on Friday 12th. July. On the following day both the **BRITANNIA** and the **GLEN GOWER** ran afternoon cruises to Spithead for their passengers to watch the warships assembling for the review. On Sunday 14th. the **BRITANNIA** took the long day trip from Hastings, Eastbourne, Brighton and Worthing to view the fleet at Spithead, calling at Shanklin for an hour on the return journey. On Monday 15th. she again joined the **GLEN GOWER,** bound for Spithead where the latter landed passengers aboard **HMS REVENGE** and the **BRITANNIA** landed hers on **HMS HOOD.**

Review day was Tuesday 16th. July. All of the vessels visiting Spithead for the event had to be in position between specified times, on this occasion between 13.00 and 18.00, during which period they were not allowed to move from their alloted anchorages.

The **BRIGHTON QUEEN** sailed from Brighton at 09.40 for Spithead and cruised through the lines of warships before anchoring at 13.00. An hour later, the King, aboard the Royal Yacht **VICTORIA AND ALBERT**, with the Trinity House Vessel, **PATRICIA,** ahead and escorted by **HMS ENCHANTRESS,** proceeded to Spithead for the Inspection of the Fleet, which began at 15.00 and ended with a fly past of the Fleet Air Arm at 17.00. At 18.00 the **BRIGHTON QUEEN** hove up and sailed through the fleet again before arriving back at Brighton at about 20.30. The **GLEN GOWER** ran a similar trip from Eastbourne.

The **BRIGHTON BELLE** sailed from Worthing but followed a slightly different programme. After leaving Spithead at 18.00, she proceeded to Shanklin, berthing for about an hour, before returning to Spithead, arriving at 21.50, where she anchored for passengers to watch the firework display and view the illuminations. She left Spithead at 23.30, arriving back at Worthing at 02.50 on the following day.

The **BRITANNIA** was on charter for the day, to Frames Tours Ltd., who had organised a rail connection from London to Southampton, from where she sailed at 09.45. After cruising through the fleet, she also anchored from 13.00 for the review. At 18.15 she cruised through the lines again and anchored once more, at 21.15, for the illuminations and firework display. She hove up at 00.30 on Wednesday 17th. July and returned to Southampton, arriving at 01.50.

There was to be little rest for her crew. At 10.17 she sailed for the Bristol Channel, passing the Longships at 23.00 and arriving at Ilfracombe at 05.30 on Thursday 18th. July. Five hours later she was off again, on a day trip to Clovelly and Lundy Island, eventually arriving back at Cardiff at 22.30.

The company had hoped for good revenue from the review sailings and were not disappointed. Fortunately, the weather had been excellent, with sunny days and light breezes; a high spot in an otherwise, indifferent summer.

On the morning of Friday 19th. July the P. & O. passenger liner, **STRATHNAVEN,** steamed up the Bristol Channel to call off Avonmouth. The **RAVENSWOOD** sailed light from Newport early that day to act as tender, if necessary. She was not required, however, and anchored in Walton Bay until the evening when she ran a cruise from Clevedon to join the **BRITANNIA,** from Cardiff and Penarth, and the **GLEN AVON,** from Weston, to escort the liner down channel on her departure.

The **RAVENSWOOD** sustained paddle damage on an evening trip from Newport to Ilfracombe on Saturday 27th. July. The trouble occured at about 20.30, near Hurlstone Point, while she was heading into a strong wind and heavy seas. She turned around and made her way, at slow speed, to Barry, arriving at just after midnight on Sunday 28th. Repairs were effected later that day and included the replacement of several bell cranks and two radius rods. She was back in service on the following morning but, two weeks later, the bell cranks were found to be cracked and it was necessary for her to spend a few days in Bristol while further repairs were carried out.

On the South Coast, the **BRIGHTON QUEEN** ran the first ever trip to Fecamp, "The Home of Radio Normandy", on Monday 22nd. July, and on the following Sunday another innovation took place with the first, combined steamer and air trip. The **GLEN GOWER** took her passengers to Ryde, from where a limited number of sixteen, at an additional fare of one guinea, were taken on a single flight from Ryde Aerodrome to Bournemouth, returning to Ryde by coach for the journey back to Brighton. This introductory trip proved to be quite a novelty, and although it was the only such event that season, the service was to be developed in subsequent years.

The **BRIGHTON QUEEN'S** return trip to Bristol, which began on Monday 23rd. September, was accomplished without incident, but the **BRIGHTON BELLE,** for the second year running, experienced a long and frustrating journey.

"Sunday 29th. September.
22.25.   Dep. Newhaven for Bristol.
Monday 30th. September.
01.00.   Strong WSW wind and sea. Increasing to gale force.
03.00.   Hove to.
05.30.   Abeam of Owers Lightvessel. Running for shelter.
07.50.   Anchored off Ryde.
12.00.   Hove up.
13.25.   Anchored off Yarmouth. Weather too bad to proceed.
Tuesday 1st. October.
11.15.   Left Yarmouth Roads.
12.45.   Arrived at Southampton for fresh water and coal.
Wednesday 2nd. October.
07.08.   Dep. Southampton. Wind and sea increasing.
13.25.   Anchored in Portland Harbour.
Thursday 3rd. October.
10.10.   Proceeded. Heavy swell.
Friday 4th. October.
12.00.   Passed the Longships.
23.10.   Lynmouth Foreland.
Saturday 5th. October.
01.00.   Anchored in Barry Roads.
10.40.   Arrived in Bristol.
           Sailing time - 4 days, 5 hours, 50 minutes.

The steamers official log books, kept by the masters, contain the precise details of their sailings, as above, but naturally lack any kind of "personal" touch.

Fortunately, one of the passengers on the **GLEN GOWER'S** homeward trip was Mr. George Owen, whose custom it was to keep a log of all his sailings. With the accuracy of a seasoned mariner and an instinctive feeling for "atmosphere", he vividly describes the experiences of a night on the storm-tossed waters of the English Channel:-

"Monday 7th. October 1935.
09.59.   Left Palace Pier, Brighton. Sea dead calm, wind nil. About 50 aboard.
11.45.   Selsey Bill abeam. Sea same. Light heat haze in distance.
12.49.   Arrived at Ryde. Discharged 6, embarked 3.

12.56.	Left Ryde.
14.15.	Needles abeam. Streamed log, port side. Light NW wind.
15.30.	St. Alban's Head abeam. 18 nautical miles from the Needles. Ship therefore making a fraction over 15 knots. Wind backing westerly and freshening.
16.40.	Weymouth abeam. Radio warning of gale from SW.
19.40.	Berry Head, Brixham, abeam. Wind WSW, moderate.
20.15.	Start Point abeam.
21.00.	Wind WSW, fresh. Sea rising. Clouds scudding across moon.
21.50.	Eddystone abeam. Wind WSW, strong. Turned in.

Tuesday 8th. October.

00.45.	Motion of ship woke me, so came on deck. Lizard on starboard quarter. Gale from SW. Ship pitching heavily.
01.30.	Steering down towards Wolf Rock.
02.00.	Very big seas coming up. Can see white crests going past in the darkness. Ship making splendid weather of it. Not much water coming aboard but thick spray. Ship reduced to half speed. Mate and four men shifting all forward gear and seats abaft bridge. Everything snugged down. Wind screaming through stays and funnel guys
03.00.	Longships abeam to starboard. Seas very long and high.
03.15.	Rounded Longships. Course N by E. Wind still very high, howling through rigging. Wolf Rock on port quarter. Turned in.
06.15.	Trevose Head abeam. Sea still running very high. Engineers easing her down on the heavy rolls, otherwise full speed.
08.35.	Hartland Point abeam.
10.00.	Arrived at Ilfracombe.
10.30.	Left Ilfracombe.
13.10.	Arrived at Cardiff.
13.35.	Left Cardiff.
15.35.	Made fast at Hotwells Landing Stage. Disembarked. Ship passed into Cumberland Basin immediately.

Later that year, the directors report stated that the season had produced a profit of £13,397, despite the poor summer. It was also announced that Capt. Peter retired from his position as Joint Managing Director on 31st. December 1935.

The BRIGHTON BELLE in the Cumberland Basin, Bristol, after her return from re-boilering at Barrow-in-Furness. Sunday 22nd. April 1934. (ERK)

The BRIGHTON QUEEN at Bournemouth Pier, 1934. Forward of the capstan is the steering wheel for turning her bow rudder. (CCC)

The WAVERLEY, arriving at Ilfracombe in 1934. (HGO)

A rare photograph indeed! The WESTWARD HO's only peacetime visit to the Sussex coast. She is seen alongside the immobilised BRIGHTON BELLE in Newhaven harbour on the evening of Tuesday 18th. September 1934, shortly before the latter left, in tow, for Bristol. (HAA)

The BRITANNIA in the Cumberland Basin about to leave for re-boilering at Glasgow. Tuesday 5th. March 1935.
(ERK)

The BRITANNIA at Barclay & Curle's yard, Glasgow, during re-boilering. March 1935. (FP)

Nearing completion, the BRITANNIA'S new funnel has been fitted but has yet to be painted. March 1935. (FP)

Publicity leaflet issued during 1935.

BRITANNIA arriving at Ilfracombe. 1935. (HGO)

The WESTWARD HO and WAVERLEY at the Tramway Centre, Bristol, during the Silver Jubilee Celebrations.
Sunday 5th. May 1935. (ERK)

The BRIGHTON QUEEN leaving Swansea. Sunday 9th. June 1935. (HGO)

Aboard the WAVERLEY in Swansea Bay, 1935. (HGO)

The RAVENSWOOD and GLEN USK at Swansea during the 1930's. Their sailings have been cancelled for the day owing to torrential rain. (HGO)

The CAMBRIA minus her starboard paddle, laid up at Bristol in 1935. (HGO)

See the
NAVAL REVIEW

Spithead, July 16th

DESTROYERS IN LINE AHEAD   [Topical Press

"I AM PROUD OF MY NAVY"

—the words of H.M. The King after his great inspection in 1914.

Now is your chance to SEE the Navy— the Nation's Sure Shield, as the King called it.

See the Royal Naval Review yourself from the good ship "BRITANNIA." (Specially chartered by FRAMES')

This, and following page: The leaflet issued by Frames Tours for their charter of the BRITANNIA for Naval Review Day 1935.

See Britain's Navy from the "BRITANNIA"

A NAVY TO BE PROUD OF

Now we have an opportunity to see this Navy—not merely to look at a photograph or film, or hear a broadcast, but to be actually around and amongst these waspslike destroyers ; to hear the booming of the Royal Salute ; to watch the seaplanes and flying boats ; to be awed by immense lordly battleships, with their lanky throatening guns ; to move like them on the rippling green water ; to see their great bows that cleave the sea, and their powerful screws that whisk a riot of foamy wake behind them ; to feel the spray and taste salt in the air ; with a blue sky over all, blithe and gay with the colours of fluttering bunting, gleaming in the sunshine.

After dark comes the romantic climax. The whole Fleet bursts into the splendour of illuminations, every single light repeated in a thousand mirrorlike ripples, while the sea and the heavens are scoured by searchlights.

This Jubilee year Britons have shown the King that they are emphatically proud of him. Now we have a chance to join him in saying once again, "I am proud of my Navy." And we have the chance to be there.

Come with us aboard the good ship "Britannia," the flagship of the famous fleet of P. & A. Campbell's pleasure steamers.

Completely overhauled and refurnished, the "Britannia" is in practically new condition, an outstanding example of a modern pleasure steamer—in fact, a miniature liner. The photographs show two of her fine public rooms, and there is also a ladies' room and ample deck space.

The ship has wireless. Music on deck and in saloon. There will be plenty of room for everyone, for although the "Britannia" can accommodate over a thousand persons, about 550 will be booked on this day. Splendid unobstructed views from all parts of the decks.

PROGRAMME

About 160 naval vessels will be present, representing the Mediterranean, Home, and Reserve Fleets.

Tuesday, July 16th. Leave London (Waterloo Station) by special train about 8 a.m. (exact time will be confirmed later) or proceed independently to Southampton from other parts.

Shortly after arrival of the train at Southampton the "Britannia" will depart, passing many of the great and famous passenger ships which dock there, and will proceed to her specially reserved anchorage.

At 2 p.m. the King, in the Royal Yacht "Victoria and Albert," preceded by the Trinity House Yacht "Patricia," and escorted by "H.M.S. Enchantress," with members of the Admiralty on board, proceeds to Spithead.

At 4 p.m. the King inspects the Fleet, and at the end of the review the Fleet Air Arm will fly past.

At 6 p.m. the "Britannia" will leave her anchorage to proceed through the naval lines, and from 10 p.m. to midnight the Fleet will be illuminated and will give a searchlight display.

Arrive Southampton after midnight. Special train departs for London, arriving early morning.

The charge for the "Britannia" cruise will be

FROM LONDON **35/-**

FROM SOUTHAMPTON **25/-**

(Covering rail and steamer trip)   (Steamer only)

(For children there will be a reduction of 7s. 6d. in the fare from London. If booking from Southampton only, 2s. 6d. reduction.)

CATERING

Arrangements for booking for luncheon services are explained below with menus, and special attention is drawn to the three services for luncheon. For High Tea or Supper there will be no set times—continuous service from 5 p.m. onwards.

At all times, except during luncheon, a variety of refreshments at attractive prices will be available, or Plain Tea 1s. 6d. There is an excellent bar on board.

The catering can be confidently recommended. The "Britannia" is the principal ship of a fleet that takes a pride in its catering. Cooking is done by electricity.

BOOK EARLY — see addresses on back

MENUS

FOUR COURSE LUNCHEON
3.6
(Three Sittings—see centre notice.)

Salmon or Lobster Mayonnaise
Cold Roast Sirloin Beef
or Cold Corned Silverside Beef
or Cold Pressed Brisket Beef
or Cold Veal and Ham Pie
or York Ham, Ox Tongue.
Potatoes.   Salads.

Fruit Salad
or Blackcurrant Tart and Cream
or Raspberry Trifle
or Macedoine of Fruit in Jelly

Cheddar.   Gorgonzola.

N.B.—Book in advance (see centre).

BOOKING FOR MEALS

Meals should be booked in advance at time of taking tickets, to facilitate suitable arrangements.

For Luncheon there will be three services, commencing at 11.30 a.m., 12.30 p.m., and 1.30 p.m., respectively. At time of booking passengers will have the choice of first, second or third service, unless a particular service is already fully booked. The service will be denoted by the colour of the luncheon ticket.

For High Tea or Supper there will be no set time. Advance booking is desirable, however.

HIGH TEA or SUPPER
2.6
(from 5 p.m. onwards till time of landing.)

Cold Meat Salad
or Fried Fillets Plaice
or Fried Fillets Sole
or Cold Salmon

Bread and Butter
Preserves
Cake

N.B.—Book in advance (see centre).

A GRAND SHIP for a GRAND TRIP

We have chartered the smartest ship of her kind. The "Britannia" is just in commission again after thorough refitting and refurnishing.

Length, 235 feet.

Horse Power, 2,400.

Speed, 20 knots.

Photos (1) Dining Saloon (2) Lounge (3) General View

P. & A. CAMPBELL LTD.

SILVER JUBILEE
Royal Naval Review
at Spithead

By H.M. THE KING

Tuesday, 16th July, 1935

SPECIAL EXCURSION by the

BRIGHTON QUEEN

(Weather and circumstances permitting)

Leave Palace Pier 9.40 a.m.   Back about 8.30 p.m.

In accordance with official regulations the steamer will take up her allotted position at Spithead before 1 p.m., and remain until released at 6 p.m.

The REVIEW commences at 4 p.m.

CATERING.—Meals and Refreshments will be supplied at the usual tariff, and for the convenience of passengers reserved Tickets for luncheon at a definite hour may be obtained from the Purser after leaving the Pier without extra charge.

A limited number of seats on the Bridge Deck obtainable at 5/- each.

TICKETS 20/- EACH

NUMBER STRICTLY LIMITED

Now obtainable from :—

T. COOK & SON, Ltd., Bostel House, West St., B'ton (Tel. : B'ton 4363)
DEAN & DAWSON, Ltd., 89, King's Rd., Brighton { ,, ,, 3466)
PICKFORD'S TRAVEL SERVICE, 95, Queen's Road { ,, ,, 5411)
and 90, Western Road { ,, Hove 4819)

P. & A. CAMPBELL, Ltd., 25, Old Steine, Brighton.
Brighton Tel. 5478   R. F. BEARD, Agent
Telegrams : "Ravenswood," Brighton.

The Southern Publishing Co., Ltd., 130, North Street, Brighton, 21583

P. & A. CAMPBELL LTD.

FOR THE FIRST TIME !

Monday, 22nd July, 1935

Special Excursion by the

BRIGHTON QUEEN

(Weather and circumstances permitting)

to

FÉCAMP

The Home of Radio Normandy

Leave Eastbourne Pier - - 8. 0 a.m.
  ,,   Brighton Palace Pier - - 9.20 a.m.

Due Fécamp 2.0 p.m.   Leave Fécamp 5.0 p.m.
Due Eastbourne 9.15 p.m.   Due Brighton 10.40 p.m.

RETURN FARE 12/6
(CHILDREN UNDER 14, 7/6)

Allowing 3 hours ashore to visit the celebrated Benedictine Abbey, a masterpiece of Norman architecture, the Benedictine Museum containing rare and beautiful examples of Works of Art and adjoining, the laboratory for the manufacture of the famous liqueur ; also the Casino, bathing station and harbour, and to the south the Municipal Park and the charming Promenade used by the Abbey Clergy since the foundation.

IMPORTANT NOTICE.— ONLY BRITISH OR FRENCH SUBJECTS

NO PASSPORTS REQUIRED

For further information apply:

P. & A. CAMPBELL Ltd., 25, Old Steine, Brighton
R. F. BEARD, Agent   Telephone 5478

PIER, EASTBOURNE
Telephone 1690
W. A. PELLY, Agent

The Southern Publishing Co., Ltd., 130, North Street, Brighton—22153

The GLEN GOWER at Shanklin. 1935. (HGO)

The BRITANNIA and BRIGHTON BELLE at Newhaven. Friday 12th. July 1935. (HAA)

The GLEN GOWER at Newhaven on an afternoon cruise from Brighton. To save time in turning she is being towed out of the harbour by the tug, RICHMOND. Friday 12th. July 1935. (HAA)

Tea time at Shanklin, Sunday 14th. July 1935. The holidaymakers relax in their deck chairs while the BRITANNIA simmers at the pier. (HAA)

The BRIGHTON QUEEN moves to her allotted anchorage for the Review of the Fleet. Tuesday 16th. July 1935. (CCC)

The GLEN USK at Gilchrist's Wharf, Newport. 1935. (SR)

Chapter 8 – 1936/1937

The **GLEN GOWER'S** round trip to Brighton began on Wednesday 20th. May, with Capt. Bruford in command. She was followed on Friday 22nd. by the **BRIGHTON QUEEN.** Her trip was somewhat different in that it was made earlier in the year than usual, and that it started in the evening instead of the morning. She crossed from Cardiff and Penarth to Clevedon where she picked up the Bristol round trippers who had just disembarked from the **WAVERLEY.** She then sailed direct to Ilfracombe from where, at 23.30, she set off into the night with sixty-four passengers, including Gwyneth White. It was quite a routine trip but featured two vessels in circumstances as diverse as the ships themselves. Miss White's diary states:-

> "Saturday 23rd. May 1936.
> After passing Plymouth at 11.30, everyone was on the look-out for the spot on which the ill-fated Herzogin Cecilie lies. The Brighton Queen's master, Capt. J. A. Harris,had announced his intention of varying the course so that we could get as close a view of her as possible, and he was as good as his word, going much further inshore than he otherwise would. Just west of the Salcombe estuary is a very fine stretch of high cliffs known as Bolt Head and Bolt Tail; the ship is lying towards the Tail, which one comes upon first. She was a pitiful sight in a seemingly impossible position, though a salvage ship is still standing by. The long, white hull is low down in the water and the red masts and spars have been cleared of canvas and rigging, so that everything looks tidy...."

The **HERZOGIN CECILIE** was a Finnish grain ship which, at the end of a voyage from Australia, was on her way from an anchorage off Falmouth to Ipswich. Early on the morning of Saturday 25th. April 1936 she ran ashore, in poor visibility, on the South Devon coast. Efforts to salvage her were unsuccessful, her cargo of grain became saturated with sea water but was discharged and sold as pig food. In June 1936 she was refloated and towed to nearby Starehole Beach in the hope of her being saved, but her weight shifted the sand, the vessel became hogged with her back broken and, sadly, she became a total loss. Incredible as it may seem only her cargo was insured, not the vessel herself, and she was sold for scrap as she lay, for a mere £250.

Miss White's diary continues:-

> "As we reached Southampton Water, later that afternoon, all eyes were on the look-out for the Queen Mary, but it was a little hazy and although we could make out two, big, two-funnelled ships, the triple ones of the great liner were not to be discerned".

In May 1930, at John Brown's Yard, Clydebank, the keel of a massive passenger liner ordered by Cunard, vessel No. 534, was laid. A year later work on the ship was suspended because of the depression. However, in December 1933, in the easing economic situation, the government agreed to advance £3 million for the completion of the ship, and a further £5 million on condition that a proposed sister ship should be built, and that Cunard and the White Star Line merged; both of these conditions were eventually fulfilled. In April 1934 work on No. 534 recommenced and she was launched on Wednesday 26th. September of that year as the **QUEEN MARY.** After fitting out she arrived at Southampton at the end of March 1936 for final dry-docking before running her trials during April. She was officially handed over to her owners, at Southampton, on Tuesday 12th. May and, over the next two weeks, she was visited by members of the Royal Family, Ministers of State, M.P.s and many other distinguished guests.

Her maiden voyage to New York was scheduled to begin on Wednesday 27th. May 1936, and the **BRIGHTON QUEEN** had journeyed south earlier than usual that year for the specific purpose of escorting the new liner to sea.

The **BRITANNIA,** (Capt. George), was also sent around for the occasion and arrived at Newhaven on Tuesday 26th. May.

On the morning of Wednesday 27th. the **GLEN GOWER** sailed from Hastings and Eastbourne for Southampton, while the **BRIGHTON QUEEN** and **BRITANNIA** left from Brighton to join her. The three ships then spent a few hours cruising in Southampton Water awaiting the **QUEEN MARY'S** departure. Capt. Couves took the **BRIGHTON QUEEN** right alongside the liner in the Ocean Terminal, then backed out and took her in again, stern first, to ensure that all of his passengers had a close-up view. At 16.30 tugs began manoeuvring the great Cunarder out of the dock and she proceeded down Southampton Water, escorted by an enormous flotilla of all kinds of craft. The paddle steamers followed her to off the Isle of Wight but as the **QUEEN MARY** gathered speed, one by one, they fell behind. One of the last to depart was the **BRITANNIA,** which had kept pace with her to the vicinity of the Nab Tower, before changing course for Brighton. The New Medway turbine steamer **QUEEN OF THE CHANNEL** had also taken part in the event and was returning to the Thames at the same time. The memorandum book records that, although she tried, the **QUEEN OF THE CHANNEL** "could not pass the Britannia between Southampton and Brighton". The **BRITANNIA** returned from Newhaven at 08.10 on Thursday 28th. May and arrived at Cardiff at 10.30 next day.

Having arrived on the South Coast earlier than usual, the **BRIGHTON QUEEN** was laid up in Newhaven harbour for two weeks and resumed sailing on Friday 19th. June In the meantime the **BRIGHTON BELLE** had entered service and made the first post-war sailing from Bognor Regis, with its new pier landing stage, on the afternoon of Thursday 11th. June.

She was involved in a most unusual, if not unique, occurrence on Friday 10th. July. Having lain at anchor off Hastings overnight she was approaching Eastbourne pier to start her day's sailings. Capt. Smith's report states:-

"At 08.43, ship struck by lightning, damaging foremast. Lightning flame passed through wireless room, damaging transmitter continued to engine room, slightly damaging dynamo and causing a shock to myself, Mate, Chief Engineer and Purser. Aerials fused and brought down to deck, smashing insulators. Proceeded to Newhaven for repairs."

Fortunately, no one sustained injury and she was back in service two days later.

For the first time in the inter-war years, the company experimented with four ships on the South Coast during the busiest months of 1936, and the **WAVERLEY,** (Capt. Hawken), accordingly left Cardiff for Brighton in time to begin sailing on Friday 17th. July.

Meanwhile, the Bristol Channel season had proceeded without incident. The **CAMBRIA** had re-entered service, after her year out of commission for overhaul, on Saturday 18th. July, resplendent with her new elliptical funnel and deckhouse. Her accommodation had also been refurbished on the same pattern as the **BRITANNIA** and **WESTWARD HO.**

The steamers' log books contain the exact details of their sailings, and those still in existence are a source of invaluable and accurate information - for the most part. However, they were not above human error. A case in point is the **CAMBRIA'S** log for Wednesday 12th. August 1936, which is reproduced on Page 172, and is worthy of closer scrutiny.

She had been off service on the previous day and left Bristol at 02.54 to anchor off Weston in readiness for her day's sailings. She is then shown as leaving Weston at 10.04 and arriving at Minehead at 10.46. The distance between the two resorts is twenty nautical miles, give or take a few cables, depending on her exact course. To cover that distance in the forty-two minutes indicated would mean that she was travelling at a speed of just over 28 knots! The **CAMBRIA** was, without doubt, a fast ship but such a speed is entirely beyond the bounds of credibility. It is obvious that the mate, who recorded the times, wrote 10.46 instead of 11.46. This would give a passage time of one hour and forty-two minutes, an average timing for the journey. She sailed from Minehead at 11.51, not 10.51, as shown, and called off Lynmouth at 12.58, again a normal passage time. A further mystery then arises in that her arrival at Ilfracombe is shown as 16.23, indicating over three hours for a trip which would normally take between 30 and 40 minutes. This mystery is solved by an examination of the memorandum book which reveals that the mate had missed out a trip! After leaving Lynmouth at 12.59, she proceeded to Ilfracombe, from where she departed at 14.20 on a cruise to off Lynmouth, returning to Ilfracombe in time to leave again at 16.30 for the return journey.

The mate was Mr. James Martin, a long-serving employee of Campbells, who had originally served in the Red Funnel Steamers. He had been mate in the **LADY MOYRA,** with Capt. Fred Nunn, and also in the **GLEN GOWER.** He was a fine seaman and most able officer who remained with the company until the early 1950's. Poor Mr. Martin, for him the "Glorious Twelfth" of 1936 must have been an "off" day.

On Monday 24th. August the **BRIGHTON QUEEN** sailed from Brighton and Eastbourne, and for the first and only time, made the four hour crossing to Le Treport, the French resort about twenty miles south west of the River Somme, on the borders of Normandy and Picardy. The trip allowed her 636 passengers about three hours ashore, sufficient to visit its two casinos and 16th. century church, or take the pre-arranged "autocar tour" to Eu, visiting the chateau, abbey church and Foret d'Eu.

The combined steamer and air trips, introduced during the previous season, run in conjunction with Railway Air Services, once again proved to be most popular and were extended during 1936 to Shanklin and Sandown, via Ryde Airport.

The weather that season, although marginally better than 1935, was, nevertheless, dismal. On her cross channel trips, the **BRIGHTON QUEEN** had been subjected to numerous batterings which caused continual damage. Although of a relatively minor nature, the constant cost of repairs led to a considerable drain on the company's resources.

One of her worst crossings took place in a westerly gale on the night of Sunday 6th. September. Prior to her leaving Boulogne, Capt. Couves, knowing what was in store, ordered the foredeck to be cleared of the buoyant seats and all moveable items and had them lashed down on the after deck. She sailed at 22.12, her passengers having enjoyed a long day at the French port, and was due to arrive at Brighton at 03.00 on the following morning. After an exceptionally rough trip she eventually arrived at Newhaven at 05.05 on Monday 7th., where she moored alongside the cross channel steamer, **PARIS**. All sailings that day were cancelled, enabling the **BRIGHTON QUEEN** to undergo necessary repairs which, as usual, included broken saloon windows, broken sponson ports, buckled sponson doors and damage to buoyant seats as well as the, not uncommon, replacement of crockery and glassware, and drying out of carpets and curtains. At noon she had to be moved from alongside the **PARIS** to the Railway Wharf, the swell, most unusually, running far into the harbour caused the two vessels to surge and bump against each other alarmingly. The gale swept across the whole of the southern half of the country and led to the cancellation of all trips in both channels on Tuesday 8th. September.

By 1936 the British economy was improving. The number of unemployed had fallen to below two million but certain areas of the country were still very badly affected, particularly South Wales and the North East. Nevertheless, the seaside resorts had been full to capacity, hardly able to keep up with the demand for accommodation. A small percentage of holidaymakers could afford to stay at the luxury hotels which lined the seafronts, but the majority had to take lodgings behind the promenades. The seaside landlady became a figure of folk myth and the butt of many music hall jokes. Not all of them were the harridans that they were made out to be, but many people complained about poor food and uncomfortable conditions as the maximum number of guests were crammed into the minimum amount of space. One such person was a South African showman by the name of Billy Butlin, who was so appalled by his treatment in a British holiday resort that he set up his first Holiday Camp in Skegness in 1936. There, a person could enjoy "A week's holiday for a week's pay", and never mind the weather! The idea was a success and developed so rapidly that, within three years, there were no fewer than about 200 holiday camps throughout Britain, owned by a variety of companies.

During the year a constitutional crisis erupted when, following the death of King George V in January, rumours became widespread of a liaison between his son, King Edward VlII, and American divorcee, Mrs. Wallis Simpson. After months of speculation and uncertainty, the situation came to a head on Friday 11th. December when the King abdicated, and made a moving radio speech to the nation that evening. He was succeeded by his brother, the Duke of York, whose first act as monarch was to create Edward, Duke of Windsor.

The Coronation of King George V1 was to take place on Wednesday 12th. May 1937 and was to be followed by a Naval Review in Spithead during the following week. P. & A. Campbell Ltd., as usual, lost no time in making the most of such an opportunity for good business, and ensured that the White Funnel Fleet would be well represented at the occasion.

The **WAVERLEY** and the **GLEN GOWER** went south from Cardiff on Monday 10th. May, the former leaving, light, at 08.00 and the latter, with 36 passengers, at 10.15. That evening trouble occurred. At 20.50, in Mount's Bay, the **GLEN GOWER'S** steering gear jammed and she had to proceed, at slow speed, using the emergency hand steering gear; the tiller, normally lashed to the after rail, being fitted to the rudder post at the stern. Capt. Bruford decided to make for Falmouth for repairs and at 21.35 radioed to Capt. Hawken, on the **WAVERLEY,** requesting him to turn back and stand by. The **WAVERLEY**, then near the Eddystone, immediately put about and fell in with the **GLEN GOWER** off The Lizard, at 23.45. Both ships then proceeded in the moderate SE wind and swell and arrived off Falmouth at 01.15 on Tuesday 11th. May, where the **GLEN GOWER** took a pilot on board and anchored in the harbour. The **WAVERLEY** then went alongside, trans-shipped the passengers and, at 02.20, proceeded to Brighton, where she arrived at just after 18.00.

Meanwhile, the Bristol office had been notified of the **GLEN GOWER'S** plight, and the Managing Director, Mr. W. J. Banks, having taken certain parts from the steering engine of the **WESTWARD HO,** left the Underfall Yard, by car, at 00.45 for Falmouth. He arrived at 06.10, and had the parts taken out to the **GLEN GOWER.** The ship's engineers replaced a gear wheel which had become stripped and at 12.30 she proceeded to Brighton. Both the **GLEN GOWER** and **WAVERLEY** began sailing on the following morning, Coronation Day.

The **BRIGHTON QUEEN** journeyed south on Thursday 13th. May, followed by other members of the fleet during the ensuing week:-

Friday 14th. May.
BRITANNIA, (Capt. George).
10.00   Depart Cardiff.

Saturday 15th. May.
BRITANNIA.
06.35   Arrived off Bournemouth.
09.15   Arrived at Bournemouth Pier.

Sunday 16th. May.
BRITANNIA.
13.45   Dep. Bournemouth on cruise through lines of warships in Spithead.
18.00   Arr. Bournemouth. Light to Newhaven.

Monday 17th. May.
BRITANNIA.
10.30   Dep. Brighton on cruise to Spithead.
17.35   Arr. Brighton. Light to Newhaven.

Tuesday 18th. May.
BRITANNIA.
Off service at Newhaven.
CAMBRIA, (Capt. J. A. Harris).
04.10   Dep. Cardiff for Southampton.
13.30   Passed the Longships.
GLEN USK, (Capt. George Spong).
04.25   Dep. Cardiff for Southampton.
13.50   Passed the Longships.
DEVONIA, (Capt. W. Riddell).
04.25   Dep. Swansea for Newhaven.

Wednesday 19th. May.
CAMBRIA.
03.30   Arrived off Southampton. Went to anchor off Netley.
10.00   Proceeded to berth 102.
18.00   Proceeded to berth 104.
GLEN USK.
06.00   Arrived off Southampton. Went to anchor off Netley.
10.00   Proceeded to berth 102.
18.33   Proceeded to berth 104.
DEVONIA.
07.10   Arrived at Newhaven.
BRITANNIA.
06.50   Dep. Newhaven for Southampton.
11.32   Arr. Southampton.
13.10   Dep. Southampton.
        Cruised through lines of warships.
        On charter to Cardiff Civic Authority.
        514 passengers.
17.15   Moored in Ocean Dock, Southampton.

Thursday 20th. May. Naval Review Day.
BRITANNIA.
10.00   Dep. Southampton. Cruised through the lines.
13.20   Anchored off Calshot Spit.
18.00   Cruised through the lines.
20.45   Anchored for illuminations and fireworks.
23.00   Hove up. Proceeded to Southampton.
        On charter to Frames Tours. 524 passengers.
CAMBRIA.
        Same itinerary,
        approximately,
        as **BRITANNIA.**
        On charter to Dean & Dawson.482 passengers.

GLEN GOWER.		Same itinerary,	520 passengers.
BRIGHTON QUEEN.	}	approximately,	570 passengers.
GLEN USK.		as **BRITANNIA.**	587 passengers.

All three ships on charter to T. R. Lunn.

DEVONIA.

Brighton to Spithead for Review.
On charter to Thomas Cook. 553 passengers.

WAVERLEY.

Hastings, Eastbourne and Bognor Regis
to Spithead for Review. 459 passengers.

The weather that day was perfect and the event was a great success. Mr. Thornton was aboard the **BRIGHTON QUEEN** and stated:-

"The day was somewhat enlivened by the master of the Brighton Queen vying with that of the Britannia to obtain a good viewpoint from which to see the fleet "lit up". Capt. Couves was chased away by a "snotty", (a midshipman), in a naval pinnace. Later on the Brighton Queen indulged in a spirited race against the Thames paddle steamer, Crested Eagle, back to Southampton, which, alas, the Crested Eagle won."

The great occasion was fully reported in the newspapers and on the newsreels. There was also live radio coverage, which turned out to be something of an embarrassment to the BBC. The commentator was Commander Thomas Woodroofe, who was broadcasting from one of the warships. Throughout the day he had been entertained in the wardroom by the ship's officers and, by evening, it was not only the fleet that was "lit up". Commander Woodroofe was feeling the effects of a little too much naval hospitality. Despite his rather slurred, spasmodic and repetitive commentary, and the fact that the BBC engineers were desperately trying to separate him from the microphone, in true naval tradition he carried on with determination and as much dignity as he could muster. Nevertheless, the broadcast, which was recorded and is still heard on radio from time to time, endeared itself to all those who shared the experience.

On the day after the Review the **BRITANNIA** left Southampton for Bristol; the **CAMBRIA,** for Cardiff then to Bristol to lay up for a month; and the **GLEN USK,** for Swansea. The **DEVONIA** returned from Newhaven to Bristol to lay up until the end of July, when she took over the Swansea station from the **GLEN USK.** The sailings of the three South Coast steamers were cancelled for the day, owing to heavy rain. In fact, only the **WAVERLEY** returned to service for a while; at Newhaven the **GLEN GOWER** was laid up until the end of May and the **BRIGHTON QUEEN** until mid-June.

It had been found during the previous season that the south coast traffic, while insufficient to maintain four ships, warranted the replacement of the **BRIGHTON BELLE** with the larger capacity of the **WAVERLEY.**

The somewhat inappropriately named **BRIGHTON BELLE** had entered service in the Bristol Channel for the Whitsun period, after which she returned to Bristol to lay up. When she resumed sailing on Saturday 3rd. July her appearance caused something of a shock! In addition to her new, elliptical funnel, similar to that of the **CAMBRIA,** she appeared with a light grey hull. The experiment was not a success; it gave her a "washed out" look, which few people liked and many were of the opinion that it looked like undercoat. It earned her the nickname of "The Grey Ghost".

The season continued with fine weather and relatively few problems. A few odds and ends are, however, worthy of mention - The **CAMBRIA** made cruises from Tenby, on Thursday 5th. August and Monday 6th. September, somewhat unusually, around Caldey Island, instead of the usual cruise along the coast towards the Stack Rocks; the **GLEN USK** was out of service at Cardiff from Sunday 8th. August for four days owing to engine trouble, and the **BRITANNIA** experienced problems at Lundy Island on Thursday 9th. September when an easterly wind blew up and caused great difficulty in re-embarking her passengers. She eventually departed, two hours late, having had to leave about twenty passengers behind owing to the dangerous conditions. They were accommodated on the island overnight and returned in the **CAMBRIA** on the following day.

The **RAVENSWOOD** encountered problems on Tuesday 7th. September which are fully documented in Capt. Brander's log:-

> "At Newport, channel cruise cancelled owing to strong wind and heavy rain. Proceeded light to Cardiff. At 19.46, abeam of Powder House Point Light, in the middle of the River Usk, with the two leading lights of Julians Pill in line, I had just put the engine room telegraph at Full Speed Ahead, when we heard a noise in the starboard paddle wheel. The engines were stopped at once and our starboard anchor was dropped. The Chief Engineer examined the wheel and found one paddle arm damaged and other various damage which made us unable to use the engines. We decided to try and berth alongside the Eastern Dry Dock jetty and with the aid of the flood tide and our starboard anchor we were able to sheer in. When close enough we lowered our port, after lifeboat and ran away a head and stern rope on to the jetty which enabled us to heave the steamer alongside. At 21.15 we made fast and the foreman shipwright from the Eastern Dry Dock came on board. He, the mate and the bosun were engaged throughout the night attending moorings until the steamer was settled on the mud at 02.45 on Wednesday 8th. September."

After temporary repairs she proceeded on the following morning, at slow speed, to Bristol where the problems were rectified in time for her to resume sailing on Thursday 9th.

The fine season ended when the **BRIGHTON BELLE** made the last ferry sailings on Monday 11th. October. The newspapers later summarised the directors' report for the year:-

> "P. & A. CAMPBELL PROFITS JUMP
> In their report for the year ended 31st. December 1937, the directors state that the accounts, after charging all running expenses and managing director's salary, show a profit of £26,885. The steamers have been maintained in the usual high state of efficiency. The directors state that the seven vessels at the Coronation Naval Review in May last gave complete and entire satisfaction to all charterers."

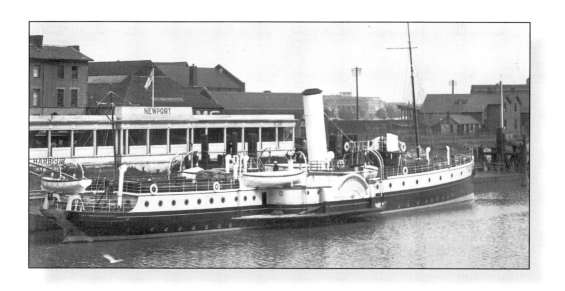

The BRIGHTON BELLE at Newport. May 1936. (CCC)

The CAMBRIA at Minehead Pier. 1936.
(CCC)

P. & A. CAMPBELL LIMITED.

SAILINGS FROM HOTWELLS, BRISTOL, 1936

(Weather and circumstances permitting),

BY THE SALOON STEAMERS

BRITANNIA, WESTWARD HO, GLEN AVON, GLEN USK,
WAVERLEY, DEVONIA, RAVENSWOOD.

SATURDAY, May 16th	Circular Trip to CLEVEDON or WESTON (out by Boat, return by Rail or Bus). Leave Bristol 3.30 p.m. Single Trip to ✱CLEVEDON, ✱WESTON, PENARTH, and ✱CARDIFF. Leave Bristol 3.30 p.m.
SUNDAY, May 17th	Afternoon CRUISE UP RIVER SEVERN to River Wye. Leave Bristol 3.0 p.m., back about 5.0 p.m. Fare 1/6. Circular Trip to CLEVEDON or WESTON (out by Boat, return by Rail or Bus). Leave Bristol 5.15 p.m. Single Trip to ✱CLEVEDON, ✱WESTON, PENARTH, and ✱CARDIFF. Leave Bristol 5.15 p.m. NOTE.—A Steamer leaves Cardiff 12.10 p.m., Penarth 12.20, Weston 1.10, Clevedon 1.45 p.m. for Bristol.
WEDNESDAY May 20th	**BRIGHTON** CIRCULAR TRIP TO BRIGHTON by P.S. " Glen Gower." Leave Bristol 7.30 a.m. per P.S. " Glen Avon " (Change at Cardiff to P.S. " Glen Gower ") Cardiff 9.45 a.m. for Ilfracombe and Brighton, due Brighton about noon on Thursday, May 21st. Fares : 15/- Single, 30/- Return. For further information see Special Bills. Single Trip to ✱CLEVEDON, ✱CARDIFF, PENARTH, and ILFRACOMBE. Leave Bristol 7.30 a.m.
FRIDAY, May 22nd	**BRIGHTON** CIRCULAR TRIP TO BRIGHTON by P.S. " Brighton Queen." Leave Bristol 7.0 p.m. per P.S. " Waverley " (change at Clevedon to P.S. " Brighton Queen "). Leave Clevedon 8.20 p.m. for Ilfracombe and Brighton, due Brighton about 9.0 p.m. on Saturday, May 23rd. Fares : 15/- Single, 30/- Return. For further particulars see Special Bills. Evening CRUISE to CLEVEDON PIER. Leave Bristol 7.0 p.m. Leave Clevedon 8.15 p.m., back about 9.15 p.m. Fare 1/6. Single Trip to CLEVEDON and ILFRACOMBE. Leave Bristol 7.0 p.m.
SATURDAY, May 23rd	Evening CRUISE UP RIVER SEVERN to River Wye, passing Sudbrook and Charstone Rock. Leave Bristol 7.45 p.m., back about 10.0 p.m. Fare 1/6.
SUNDAY, May 24th	Evening CRUISE DOWN CHANNEL, passing Portishead and to Walton Bay. Leave Bristol 8.10 p.m., back about 10.10 p.m. Fare 1/6.
MONDAY, May 25th	✱CLEVEDON, ✱CARDIFF, PENARTH, MINEHEAD, LYNMOUTH, and ILFRACOMBE. Leave Bristol 9.0 a.m. Leave Ilfracombe 4.45 p.m., Lynmouth 5.15, Minehead 6.30, Penarth 7.35, Cardiff 8.0, Clevedon 8.55 p.m.
TUESDAY, May 26th	✱CLEVEDON, ✱CARDIFF, PENARTH, MINEHEAD, LYNMOUTH, and ILFRACOMBE. Leave Bristol 9.30 a.m. Leave Ilfracombe 5.15 p.m., Lynmouth 5.45, Minehead 7.0, Penarth 8.5, Cardiff 8.30, Clevedon 9.25 p.m.
WEDNESDAY May 27th	✱CLEVEDON, ✱CARDIFF, PENARTH, MINEHEAD, LYNMOUTH, and ILFRACOMBE. Leave Bristol 10.15 a.m. Leave Ilfracombe 5.45 p.m., Lynmouth 6.15, Minehead 7.30, Penarth 8.35, Cardiff 9.0, Clevedon 9.55 pm.
THURSDAY, May 28th	✱CLEVEDON, ✱CARDIFF, PENARTH, MINEHEAD, LYNMOUTH, and ILFRACOMBE. Leave Bristol 11.0 a.m. Leave Ilfracombe 6.0 p.m., Lynmouth 6.30, Minehead 7.45, Penarth 8.50, Cardiff 9.15, Clevedon 10.10 p.m.
FRIDAY, May 29th	Single Trip to ✱CLEVEDON, ✱CARDIFF, PENARTH, MINEHEAD, LYNMOUTH, and ILFRACOMBE. Leave Bristol 12.0 noon. Single Trips to ✱CLEVEDON, PENARTH, and ✱CARDIFF. Leave Bristol 2.0 p.m. and 3.15 p.m.
SATURDAY, May 30th	Afternoon Trip to ✱CLEVEDON, ✱CARDIFF, PENARTH, ✱BARRY PIER, MINEHEAD, LYNMOUTH, and ILFRACOMBE. Leave Bristol 1.15 p.m. Leave Ilfracombe 7.30 p.m., Lynmouth 8.0, Minehead 9.30, Barry Pier 10.30, Penarth 10.55 p.m., Cardiff 11.15 p.m., Clevedon 12.10 midnight. Afternoon CRUISE DOWN CHANNEL, passing Portishead and to Walton Bay. Leave Bristol 2.15 p.m., back about 4.20 p.m. Fare 1/6. Afternoon Trip to ✱CLEVEDON and ✱BARRY PIER. Leave Bristol 4.45 p.m. Leave Barry Pier 10.30 p.m., Clevedon 12.10 midnight. Afternoon Trip to ✱CLEVEDON, ✱CARDIFF, and PENARTH. Leave Bristol 4.35 p.m. Leave Penarth 10.55 p.m., Cardiff 11.15, Clevedon 12.10 midnight. Return Fares this day : Clevedon 2/-, Cardiff or Penarth or Barry Pier 3/6, Minehead 5/-, Lynmouth or Ilfracombe 6/-. Circular Trip to WESTON (out by Boat, return by Rail or Bus). Leave Bristol 4.45 p.m. NOTE.—A Steamer leaves Cardiff 10.50 a.m., Penarth 11.0, Clevedon 11.55 a.m. for Bristol. A Steamer also leaves Cardiff 2.0 p.m., Penarth 2.10, Clevedon 3.10 p.m., for Bristol.
WHIT SUNDAY, May 31st	Afternoon CRUISE UP RIVER SEVERN to off River Wye, thence passing the Denny and to off Battery Point. Leave Bristol 3.0 p.m., back about 5.30 p.m. Fare 2/-. Single Trip to ✱CLEVEDON, PENARTH, and ✱CARDIFF. Leave Bristol 5.40 p.m. NOTE.—A Steamer leaves Cardiff 12.30 p.m., Penarth 12.40, Clevedon 1.40 p.m., for Bristol.
WHIT MONDAY, June 1st	Long Day Trip to ILFRACOMBE. Leave Bristol 6.0 a.m. Leave Ilfracombe 11.30 p.m. for Bristol. Long Day Trip to CARDIFF, PENARTH, and BARRY PIER. Leave Bristol 6.5 a.m. Leave Barry Pier 12.30 midnight, Penarth 12.55 a.m. Tuesday, Cardiff 1.15 a.m. Tuesday. Afternoon CRUISE DOWN CHANNEL, passing Portishead and to Clevedon Pier. Leave Bristol 3.45 p.m., back about 6.0 p.m. Fare 2/-. Single Trips to CLEVEDON. Leave Bristol 3.45 p.m. and 6.15 p.m. Evening Trip to CARDIFF, PENARTH, and BARRY PIER. Leave Bristol 6.15 p.m. Leave Barry Pier 12.30 midnight, Penarth 12.55 a.m. (Tuesday), Cardiff 1.15 a.m. (Tuesday). Return Fares this Trip : Cardiff, Penarth or Barry Pier 3/6. Single Trip to ILFRACOMBE. Leave Bristol 6.15 p.m. NOTE.—A Steamer leaves Cardiff 3.30 a.m. for Bristol. A Steamer also leaves Ilfracombe 10.30 a.m., Barry Pier 12.45 p.m., Penarth 1.5, Cardiff 1.30, Clevedon 2.25 p.m., for Bristol. **NO CIRCULAR TRIP BOOKINGS THIS DAY.**

The Bristol City Line cargo vessel, MONTREAL CITY passing the GLEN GOWER at Hotwells Landing Stage.
Saturday 16th. May 1936. (ERK)

Aboard the Cunard liner, QUEEN MARY, about to leave Southampton on her maiden voyage to New York.
Wednesday 27th. May 1936. The BRIGHTON QUEEN waits astern of her at the Ocean Terminal. (CCC)

The BRITANNIA and the Southern Railway P.S. WHIPPINGHAM, escort the QUEEN MARY in Southampton Water. Wednesday 27th. May 1936. (CCC)

Dwarfed by the huge Cunarder, the BRITANNIA, BRIGHTON QUEEN and GLEN GOWER in the Solent. (CCC)

The BRITANNIA at speed off the Isle of Wight, keeping pace with the QUEEN MARY as all the other escorts fall behind. (CCC)

The WESTWARD HO and BRITANNIA at Barry. Tuesday 2nd. June 1936. (ERK)

Paddle box of the BRITANNIA in the 1930's. (ERK)

12 WEDNESDAY (225—141)
Grouse Shooting begins   HW. 2.51.   am
7½ 23'8" 3.30.   pm

arr   Dep
        Bristol   2 54 am
anchored 4.36   Weston Bay.
Hove up. 9 53.   "   10.4.   "
10.46.   Minehead.   10 51. "
12.58. Lynmouth.   12 59 pm.
4.23   Combe.   4.30. "
6.24.   Minehead.   6.31. "
7.40.   Barry   7.45. "
8.55.   Clevedon.   9.5. "
9.45.   Avonmouth.

@ Weston   Boat and Fire drill No 3. Boat.
swung out.

Strong Wly wind. Heavy Sea. Clear weather.

150 miles

J.G. Harris
master

The log of the CAMBRIA with the missing trip! (see Page 161)

172

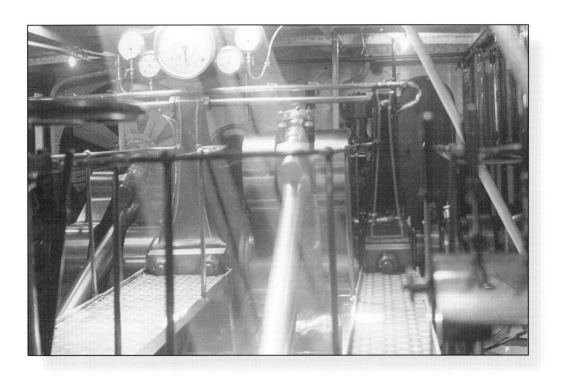

Edwin Keen's magnificent study of the CAMBRIA'S engine room, taken at Ilfracombe on Saturday 15th. August 1936. The mid-day sun streams through the open skylight, dramatically illuminating the gleaming metalwork.

The CAMBRIA leaving Ilfracombe for a cruise to Bideford Bay. Saturday 15th. August. 1936. (ERK)

The BRITANNIA arrives off Lynmouth to pick up her boat-load of passengers. Capt. George is at the telegraphs, the passengers line the starboard side to watch the embarkation, while the officers and crew wait on the after sponson to help the Lynmouth passengers aboard. 1936. (HGO)

Seagulls follow the BRITANNIA as she steams up the North Devon coast on an evening in 1936. (HGO)

214
BILLS DUE WITH GRACE
30 Days—Sept. 4
60 Days—Oct. 4
90 Days—Nov. 3

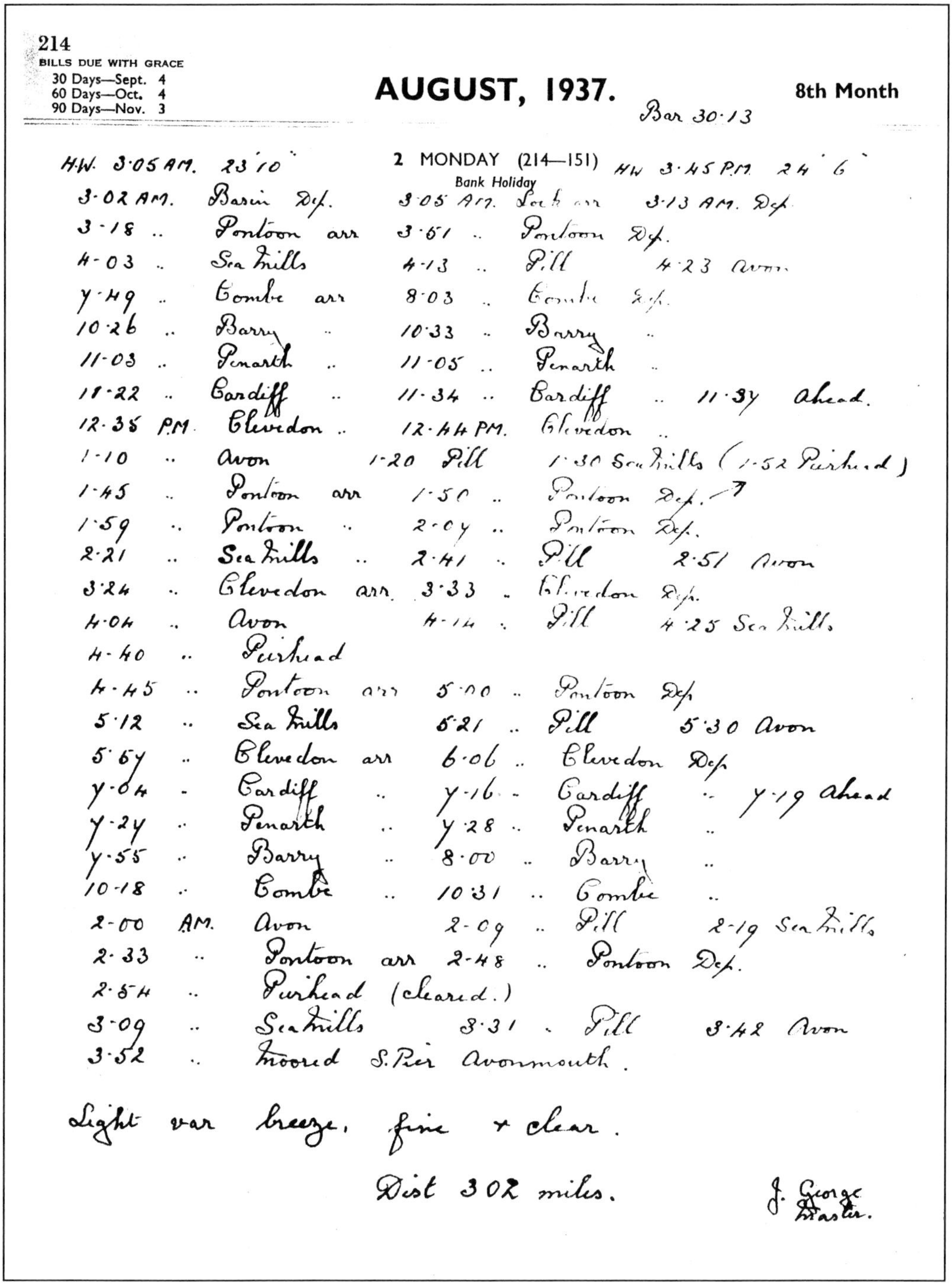

AUGUST, 1937. Bar 30·13 **8th Month**

H.W. 3·05 AM. 23' 10" **2 MONDAY (214—151)** Bank Holiday H.W. 3·45 P.M. 24' 6"

3·02 AM. Basin Dep. 3·05 AM. Lock arr 3·13 AM. Dep.
3·18 .. Pontoon arr 3·51 .. Pontoon Dep.
4·03 .. Sea Mills 4·13 .. Pill 4·23 Avon
7·49 .. Combe arr 8·03 .. Combe Dep.
10·26 .. Barry .. 10·33 .. Barry ..
11·03 .. Penarth .. 11·05 .. Penarth ..
11·22 .. Cardiff .. 11·34 .. Cardiff .. 11·37 ahead.
12·35 P.M. Clevedon .. 12·44 P.M. Clevedon ..
1·10 .. Avon 1·20 Pill 1·30 Sea Mills (1·52 Pierhead)
1·45 .. Pontoon arr 1·50 .. Pontoon Dep.
1·59 .. Pontoon .. 2·07 .. Pontoon Dep.
2·21 .. Sea Mills .. 2·41 .. Pill 2·51 Avon
3·24 .. Clevedon arr 3·33 .. Clevedon Dep.
4·04 .. Avon 4·14 .. Pill 4·25 Sea Mills
4·40 .. Pierhead
4·45 .. Pontoon arr 5·00 .. Pontoon Dep
5·12 .. Sea Mills 5·21 .. Pill 5·30 Avon
5·57 .. Clevedon arr 6·06 .. Clevedon Dep
7·04 .. Cardiff .. 7·16 .. Cardiff .. 7·19 ahead
7·24 .. Penarth .. 7·28 .. Penarth ..
7·55 .. Barry .. 8·00 .. Barry ..
10·18 .. Combe .. 10·31 .. Combe ..
2·00 AM. Avon 2·09 .. Pill 2·19 Sea Mills
2·33 .. Pontoon arr 2·48 .. Pontoon Dep.
2·54 .. Pierhead (cleared.)
3·09 .. Sea Mills 3·31 .. Pill 3·42 Avon
3·52 .. Moored S. Pier Avonmouth.

Light var breeze, fine + clear.

Dist 302 miles.

J. George
Master.

The log of the BRITANNIA for Bank Holiday Monday 2nd. August 1936. An arduous, 24 hour working day.

The RAVENSWOOD at Newport. 1936. (CCC)

The GLEN GOWER at Boulogne, 1936. (HGO)

176

The GLEN GOWER arriving at Palace Pier, Brighton, for the return trip to Bristol. Monday 5th. October 1936. (HGO)

The BRIGHTON BELLE alongside the Underfall Yard after her Easter sailings in 1937. The outer casing of her funnel has been removed but she retains her conventional hull colours. (ERK)

By Sunday 18th. June 1937 the BRIGHTON BELLE'S hull had been painted grey but the new funnel has yet to be fitted. Her radio installation and jigger have been shipped into the CAMBRIA, lying alongside. (ERK)

The BRIGHTON BELLE off Weston in 1937. In poor visibility she was difficult to see and the grey hull experiment lasted only for the one season. (ERK)

The WESTWARD HO in the Avon. Sunday 1st. August 1937. (ERK)

The BRIGHTON QUEEN in Folkestone harbour. 1937. (CCC)

Chapter 9 – 1938/1939

Before the 1938 season began the company was engaged to run a charter trip in connection with the centenary celebrations of Isambard Kingdom Brunel's paddle steamship, **GREAT WESTERN.** On the morning of Friday 8th. April, 100 years to the day on which she sailed on her maiden voyage to America, the Lord Mayor of Bristol and his guests boarded the **BRITANNIA** at Bush's Corner, Prince Street, close to the site of Patterson's yard, where the **GREAT WESTERN** was built. Shortly after noon she sailed down the Floating Harbour, through the Cumberland Basin and out of the River Avon to discharge her 228 passengers in the locks at Avonmouth, where they attended a luncheon held in one of the baggage sheds of the Royal Edward Dock rail terminal.

The season began on Wednesday 13th. April when the **BRIGHTON BELLE,** under the command of Capt. Findlay Brander, opened the Cardiff to Weston ferry. To the relief of everyone the steamer appeared in the traditional Campbell colours; the grey hull experiment had been a failure, never to be repeated. Her appearance had altered slightly, however, in that she had new paddle box facings. The concentric louvres and central emblem depicting the Virgin Mary had been replaced with horizontal slats and an emblem containing the company's houseflag. It was less aesthetically pleasing, perhaps, but more in keeping with the designs of the time.

Other changes took place that year which affected most of the steamers. The Board of Trade no longer required them to carry sails; accordingly they were removed from most of the vessels although others retained them until the outbreak of the war. However, the Board introduced another regulation which necessitated the fitting of canvas weather cloths around the steamers' forward rails, in order to protect the passengers, to some extent, from the wind and spray. This requirement was unpopular with certain masters, in particular Capt. Jack George, who often complained that the extra wind resistance slowed the **BRITANNIA** down by at least half a knot! Nevertheless, Capt. George and the **"BRIT"** remained a formidable combination, responsible for many fast passages. For example, shortly before the war she made the trip from Bristol to Cardiff, including a stop at Weston, in rapid time; she passed the Outer Wrack buoy, in Cardiff Roads, a mere 1 hour 48 minutes after leaving Hotwells Landing Stage.

The **WAVERLEY,** under the command of Capt. Fuller, left Cardiff for the South Coast on Monday 30th. May. Her departure from Ilfracombe was delayed by five hours owing to bad weather but she arrived in Newhaven on the following afternoon despite particularly heavy seas during most of the journey.

The **GLEN GOWER** was not so fortunate on her trip south. After sailing from Cardiff and Ilfracombe on Wednesday 1st. June, she was abeam of Trevose Head at 18.00 in a fresh SSE wind and moderate sea. At 18.30 the wind suddenly veered and blew from the NW, increasing to hurricane force. The log book continues:-

"18.50.   Hauled ship's head to wind, no improvement.
            Heavy sea rising. Turned ship and set course for Lundy.
20.00.   Forward port lifeboat washed clear of chocks, lowered and lashed to deck.
22.30.   Found inner frame of hawse pipe washed inboard flooding chain locker.

Forward port wing doors pushed in.

24.00.   Heavy seas. Proceeding at 'Slow' speed.

The **GLEN GOWER** anchored in Lundy Roads at 02.20 on Thursday 2nd. June. The weather conditions remained the same after daybreak and at 10.00 she was ordered to proceed to Swansea for repairs, arriving at 14.30 and discharging 17 passengers. She left Swansea at 08.30 on Friday 3rd. June and arrived at Brighton at 09.00 on the following day.

Behind the scenes, events were taking something of an unusual turn. An interesting item appears in the minute book for Tuesday 26th. July which states that Mr. Banks was granted permission by the board to make inquiries regarding the purchase of "a more suitable steamer" for the continental sailings.

It appears that the **BRIGHTON QUEEN,** although well able to handle the existing traffic, was considered a little out of date in comparison with other cross channel vessels. Additionally, with more and more people making the cross-channel trips a somewhat larger ship was advisable. Furthermore, even when running full to capacity, the **BRIGHTON QUEEN'S** large appetite for coal remained a financial drawback.

The similar situation with regard to the **DEVONIA'S** fuel consumption had led to her seasons becoming shorter as the years progressed. In 1938, under the command of Capt. George Spong, she began her Swansea sailings as late as Friday 29th. July. On Monday 5th. September she made what was to be the last visit of a Campbell steamer to Padstow for many years, and two days later made her last ever civilian sailings.

The **BRIGHTON QUEEN** and **WAVERLEY'S** return trips to Bristol passed uneventfully but, once again, the **GLEN GOWER** was on the receiving end of some very nasty weather which led to a very long journey, fully chronicled by Mr. George Owen:-

"Monday 3rd. October.

09.02.   Left Palace Pier. Wind WNW, fresh, sea moderate.
          About 50 passengers aboard.
10.45.   Wind backing to SW and freshening.
11.20   Selsey Bill abeam. Rain squalls.
11.50.   Passed German liner, "Europa", to port.
          Sea abeam, spray coming aboard.
12.18.   Warner Lightvessel abeam. Sea smooth under lee of Isle of Wight.
          Destroyer "Vega" passed to port.
12.40.   Arrived at Ryde. Disembarked 28, embarked 5.
12.45.   Left Ryde. SW cone hoisted. Went below for lunch.
13.30.   Foredeck cleared of seats and all other moveable gear, except rail seats.
13.45.   Wind SW, rising rapidly.
14.00.   Strong SW gale. Hove to off Yarmouth, Isle of Wight.
          Dropped anchor. Wireless warning of severe SW gale, probably at least
          75mph velocity. All forward rail seats shifted aft.
14.15.   Wind still rising. Lashing down all ropes and gear between funnels.
          Admiralty cable vessel, coasting schooner and steam coaster anchored in
          company.

14.35.   Southampton pilot cutter ran in for shelter.
         Blowing whole gale now from SW.
16.00.   Whole gale continuing. Anchor dragging, mate and bosun taking up a few
         links in cable. Thick mist.
16.30.   Drifted down about ½ mile. Hove up anchor, went ahead again and
         dropped anchor afresh, further under lee of land.
20.00   Whole gale continuing. Ship rolling heavily at anchor, even under lee of
         land.
22.00.   Turned in.
Tuesday 4th. October.
07.00.   Very heavy gale blowing with terrific squalls.
         Clear sky now, a bad sign of more wind.
08.00.   No Channel Island boat this tide. Lymington to Yarmouth ferry cancelled.
         Nothing from Southampton.
         Fishguard Radio Station asking for news of us.
14.00.   Hove up anchor and made for Southampton.
15.45.   Arrived at Southampton.
22.00.   Wind moderating slightly.
Wednesday 5th. October.
07.00.   Wind increased during night. Whole gale.
12.00.   Commenced coaling, also taking on water and provisions.
15.00.   Left Southampton. Wind Westerly, strong.
15.30.   Making all gear fast.
16.35.   Off Yarmouth. Wind WNW, strong.
17.05.   Needles abeam. Pitching heavily, high sea.
17.15.   Put about.
18.00.   Anchored off Yarmouth.
21.00.   Strong gale from WSW continuing overnight.
Thursday 6th. October.
06.45   Hove up anchor and put to sea. Wind NW, fresh.
07.15.   Needles abeam. High seas, pitching heavily.
08.40   St. Albans Head abeam. Heavy sea. Ship riding nicely.
09.00.   Wind Westerly and rising. Crew lashing down rails where they open up;
         lashing down anchors; after sponson doors closed; all ropes and gear on
         stern brought up and secured abaft reserve deck; all ropes and gear on
         foredeck secured between funnels; gangways lashed down.
10.15.   Portland Bill abeam. Flotilla of destroyers crossed our bows, pitching
         heavily and shipping green seas.
10.20.   Passed through the race and shipped a nasty one.
14.00.   Start Point abeam. Wind rising.
16.15.   Eddystone abeam. Wind still rising.
16.45.   Radio warning of further SW gale. Capt. Bruford determined to get around
         before it becomes too bad.
19.40.   Lizard abeam. Wind SW, rising rapidly.
21.30.   Longships abeam. Some big seas rolling up.
21.40.   Rounded Longships, rolling heavily.

| 22.10. | Pendeen abeam. Wind still rising. Rolling heavily. |
| | A dirty night, blowing hard. |

Friday 7th. October.

05.15.	Bull Point abeam. Heavy sea running. Standing well off shore.
05.30.	Off Ilfracombe, about 5 miles.
07.00.	Foreland abeam.
08.15.	Anchored off Minehead to await tide.
13.05.	Hove up anchor and made for Cardiff.
	A very heavy sea running even up here.
14.35.	Arrived at Cardiff.
16.55.	Arrived at Bristol. 4 days, 7 hours, 53 minutes from Palace Pier, Brighton.
Notes.	Wind velocities, 3/4 October.
	Lizard, 85mph., Isles of Scilly, 88mph., Pembroke, 104mph.
	2000 trees blown down in New Forest.
	Bathing huts smashed and sea front badly damaged in Bournemouth.
	Tailor's shop front blown out in Southampton and dummies blown up the the street; people thought they were bodies.
	Widespread damage over the whole of the country. Many people killed by falling trees etc.
	Kelly's coaster "Crewhill", bound from London to Douglas with cement, struck by a huge sea off the Longships which smashed the bridge and washed the master overboard. Three lifeboats carried away, put into Swansea for shelter and repairs.

This dreadful round trip marked the culmination of a poor season in which wet and windy weather had been all too prevalent. The year had also been marked by misfortune with the deaths of three of the company's most respected masters, Capt. Joe Ashford, Capt. Edward Calvert and Capt. Allan Livingstone.

Its ultimate tragedy, however, was the sudden and unexpected death of Capt. Peter Campbell on Sunday 18th. December, four days after his 80th. birthday. The newspapers mourned his loss and were lavish in their praise of his well known and popular personality:-

"Capt. Peter Campbell, one of the founders of Messrs P. & A. Campbell Ltd., died unexpectedly yesterday at his home, The Lakes, Wooton-Under-Edge...

Capt. Campbell seemed in the best of health, and on Friday night was playing his usual excellent game of billiards at his home with his son-in-law, Capt. Gordon Fry.

'Last Wednesday,' said Capt. Fry, 'we held his 80th. birthday party. There were about forty of us and I think he received enough tobacco and cigars to last him another lifetime'.

On Saturday, however, he was taken ill and his doctor was summoned, but he passed peacefully away early yesterday morning.

His death will be mourned in all those Bristol Channel ports and south coast resorts where his big, hearty figure and breezy manner were once familiar features of the holiday season.

Mr. W. J. Banks told a reporter, 'Ask anyone what they thought of Capt. Peter and they will all tell you that he was one of the finest seamen who ever stepped aboard a ship. Not only did he hold a master's certificate but also a chief engineer's ticket. What that man could not do with a paddle boat, no man could do. It did not matter to him whether he was on the bridge or in the engine room. He was equally at home.'

Capt. Peter was born at Garelochead, Dumbartonshire, in 1858, and was educated at Kilblain Academy, Greenock, and Glasgow Academy. In 1874 he was apprenticed to engineering with Messrs. W. King & Co. of Glasgow and went to sea as a marine engineer in 1881. He was engineer aboard the steamer "Strathleven", the first ship to bring frozen meat from Australia. He spent many years at sea before entering the career which brought him to Bristol in 1890...

He was a keen Rugby player in his younger days and in later years he became an enthusiastic game shot and an occasional fisherman. He was also a past president of the Caledonian Society and had been an engineer assessor to the local Marine Board.

He was also a member of the Moira Lodge of Freemasons in Bristol and a man of considerable generosity in an unostentatious way."

It had often been stated by Peter and Alec that as long as they were involved with the company, they would entertain no form of excursion vessels other than paddle steamers; their virtues far outweighing those of screw driven ships for the nature of their services. Their light draught rendered them eminently suitable for the shallow and often crowded waters of the rivers, estuaries and harbours in which they frequently performed their duties, and their manoeuvrability allowed for a rapid turn around at the landing places. Both of these attributes combined to give greater operational freedom which, in turn, led to the vessels being more fully utilised, thus giving them greater revenue potential.

The company's three south coast agents, A. J. McNair of Hastings, W. A. Pelly of Eastbourne and J. B. McDougall of Brighton had been pressing for some time for a new paddle steamer with more sheltered accommodation, in the form of sun-lounges, on their promenade decks.Mr. Banks, however, had other ideas. As already stated the board had sanctioned his proposal to acquire a more up-to-date vessel for the cross-channel sailings. He cast envious eyes over the large, modern screw vessels running to France and felt that such an addition to the White Funnel Fleet would be a distinct advantage in attracting the public to the Continental sailings. With the death of Capt. Peter he now had a clear field in which to persuade the directors of the desirability of this type of ship.

The merits and de-merits of his proposition gave rise to considerable debate. Some felt that Mr. Banks was right; that perhaps Peter and Alec had been too set in their ways and it was time for the company to move forward and modernise its fleet.

There was no doubt that the vessel would add greatly to the company's, and Mr. Banks's prestige, a factor with which he was much preoccupied. However, from the operational point of view, many argued against his proposal.

The ships to which Mr. Banks referred ran on their regular routes, in both summer and winter, constituting a service sustained by the travelling public to and from the French ports on a more "commercial" basis. Campbell's cross-channel sailings were a different matter, tapping the day excursion passengers on holiday at the south coast resorts. Furthermore, it was necessary for their vessels to call at four piers en route to the Continent in order to obtain the requisite number of passengers to make the service financially viable; the West Pier and Palace Pier at Brighton, Eastbourne and Hastings. While these calls were accomplished quickly by the paddle steamers, with a large, screw-driven vessel berthing would inevitably be a more laborious process, extending the journey by a considerable time. In order to provide the passengers with a reasonable period ashore in France, the trip would need to start early and end late, outside the optimum hours for the holidaymakers.

The minutes of the board meeting of Wednesday 15th. February state:

> "The question of placing an order for a new, twin-screw, turbine steamer for service on the south coast was discussed. Mr. Banks reported that he had obtained quotations for a suitable vessel from Charles Hill & Sons., of £113,500, and from the Ailsa Shipbuilding Co., of £112,000. Mr. Boucher also reported that the Westminster Bank were prepared to place £100,000 at the disposal of the company for the new steamer. All the members having expressed their opinion that the increase in cross-channel traffic warranted a larger and more up to date steamer, it was eventually unanimously agreed that the company should proceed with the new vessel. The board also decided that in view of certain technical points, the actual placing of the contract should be left to the discretion of Mr. Banks."

It is understood that much heated argument occurred at the meeting, not least because of the large financial committment. However, the decision had been made and the order was placed with the Ailsa Shipbuilding Co., the contract being signed and sealed on Wednesday 10th. May. A few days later a further meeting was held, at which the board were given details of the complex financial arrangements.

Whether or not the decision was the right one, only time would tell. The whole enterprise, however, was destined to be overtaken by events and the steamer's entry into the company's service lay far in the future.

In the meantime the 1939 season had begun under a cloud of uncertainty. The deteriorating situation in Europe was a cause of great concern, nevertheless, the sailings progressed satisfactorily in the fair weather.

The **BRIGHTON QUEEN'S** cross-channel trips were well patronised. The occasional trips to Fecamp and Trouville had been discontinued, Boulogne and Calais were the only French destinations during that season. On Thursday 22nd. June she sailed from Brighton to Southampton to witness the arrival of the Canadian Pacific liner, **EMPRESS OF BRITAIN.** It was a particularly special occasion, as the Brighton press reported:-

> "Among the cheering crowds who welcomed the King and Queen home from their visit to America and Canada were nearly 700 passengers aboard the White

Funnel steamer, Brighton Queen. The weather was not good, the sky was leaden-grey and at times the atmosphere was so misty that the shore could not be seen....

It was not long after the Brighton Queen had steamed past Ryde Pier that the Empress of Britain was sighted and as the bow of the Brighton ship cut through the water, the far-off image of the Royal liner became clearer until the mammoth hull and tall yellow funnels could be seen distinctly...

Soon the sturdy tugs had completed their work and the Empress of Britain was safely berthed in Southampton Dock. All this activity was watched by the passengers on board the Brighton Queen and her master, Capt. Couves, navigated the ship so skilfully that for a considerable time everybody had a close and uninterrupted view of the great liner as she lay at her berth, and eager eyes scanned the deck for a glimpse of the King and Queen.

As the bells of the town rang out a welcome to Their Majesties the Brighton Queen turned and set her course for Brighton, her passengers happy in the knowledge that they had played some part in an historic event."

The **BRIGHTON QUEEN'S** South Coast consorts were once again the **GLEN GOWER,** with Capt. Bruford in command, and the **WAVERLEY,** under the command of her former chief officer, Capt. F. A. Smyth, the son of Campbell's Swansea agent, Arthur Smyth.

In the Bristol Channel, on Tuesday 20th. June, the **CAMBRIA** ran a charter trip for a party of Bristol Docks officials similar to that of the **BRITANNIA** during the previous season. She sailed from Bush's Corner, Prince Street, down the Floating Harbour and out into Walton Bay before landing the party at Avonmouth. She was due to lay up again for a short while but re-entered service on Wednesday 21st. June to replace the **RAVENSWOOD** for a couple of days while the latter was undergoing paddle repairs.

The **DEVONIA** was towed to Avonmouth for painting on Friday 14th. July but after leaving dry dock she remained at Avonmouth and did not, in fact, enter service at all during that summer for economic reasons. The **WESTWARD HO** took her place at Swansea for the whole of the season, under the command of Capt. Horace Rumsam.

From Tuesday 4th. July there were no further calls made at Mumbles. While berthing on the previous night the **WESTWARD HO** damaged one of the pier piles, most of which were rotten. The pier company demanded that P. & A. Campbell should pay for its repair; they refused as they were paying the necessary dues and consequently did not call again.

The season continued without incident until the end of August, when events took a turn which brought the services to an abrupt, but not entirely unexpected end. In order to put matters into perspective it is necessary to retrace our steps to 1919.

After the end of the Great War the Treaty of Versailles imposed severe constraints, financial and territorial, on Germany. The Allies' conditions for surrender were deeply resented by her people and provided a fertile breeding ground for the rise of the Nazi party during the 1920's and 1930's. For many of the German people the party, with its nationalistic ideals, represented the only way for the nation to regain its pride and identity.

However, under its tyrannical leader, Adolf Hitler, the country substantially re-armed, and reclaimed not only the land ceded to her neighbours under the terms of the peace treaty but, without compunction, gradually began to seize additional territory on the pretext of "protection".

By the late 1930's Europe was riven by political and military tension. Great Britain and France, anxious to avoid another full scale conflict, pursued their policies of appeasment culminating in the Munich Agreement of September 1938, when the British Prime Minister, Neville Chamberlain, after several meetings with Hitler, proclaimed "Peace for our time". Hitler's promises meant nothing and in the face of more and more German expansionism, the stage was set for the conflict which had to come.

The BRITANNIA at Avonmouth, during the GREAT WESTERN Centenary Celebrations. Friday 8th. April 1938.
(CCC)

A busy evening at Weston Pier. The GLEN USK backs out as the BRITANNIA arrives. The GLEN AVON waits her turn offshore. Friday 13th. May 1938. (ERK)

Shortly after, the BRITANNIA leaves and the BRIGHTON BELLE arrives. The GLEN AVON has weighed anchor and prepares to make her approach. (ERK)

This, and next 2 pages: Publicity leaflet issued in the late 1930's.

ATTRACTIVE FARES

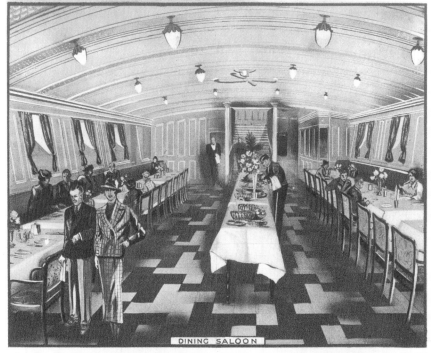

DINING SALOON

EFFICIENCY AND COMFORT

*These illustrations
speak for themselves*

"THE SIGN OF A GOOD TIME"

A REAL HOLIDAY

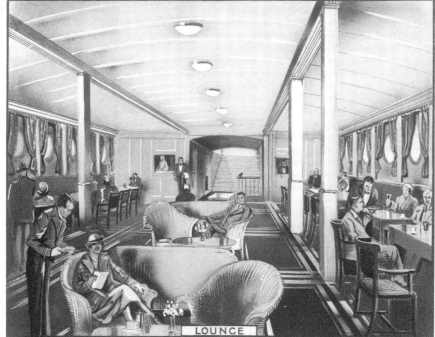

LOUNGE

REFRESHMENT BAR

The BRIGHTON QUEEN has spent the night at anchor off Brighton, but, owing to a SW gale and heavy seas, she has been ordered to enter Newhaven harbour for shelter, her sailings cancelled for the day. 1938. (HAA)

The BRIGHTON QUEEN and GLEN GOWER stormbound at Newhaven in 1938. (HAA)

191

31 Days **JULY, 1938** **29th Week**

10 Sunday (191—174) Bar 29.72
4th after Trinity

Fresh Westerly wind rough sea & overcast
7.15 a.m. Dep Newhaven
7.29 . Breakwater
8.18 . Arr Palace Pier 9.02 a.m. dep
10.05 . Beachy Head
10.19 . " Eastbourne 10.23 " "
11.10 . . Hastings 11.15 "
11.22 . Fish Quay Streamed & set log
0.15 P.m. Dungeness 9/13 log 13.1
0.56 . Varne L.V. log 25.1
2.03 - No 1 buoy hauled in log 40
2.05 . Slowed Engines awaiting signal to enter Strong SW wind
2.38 . Arr Calais 5.35 P.m. dep
5.40 Pier Head log streamed & set
5.48 . No 1 buoy log 2.3
6.53 . Spar buoy log 18.4
7.10 . Varne L.V log 21.8 Strong Wly wind rough
8.12 . Dungeness log 33. Sea half speed.
9.40 . Arr Hastings 9.50 P.m dep
10.45 . . Eastbourne 11.28 " .
11.35 . Vd off Eastbourne

On Return trip from Calais experienced very heavy weather ship labouring heavily speed half & slow at intervals had to take in canvas weather Cloth forward owing to damage to rails. tiles in lavatory washed adrift

Dist 156 Miles
W.A. Conner
Master
[signature] C/O.

From the BRIGHTON QUEEN'S log book, showing one of her two trips to Calais in 1938, accomplished in severe weather.

Looking down on the RAVENSWOOD at Barry Pier. Saturday 16th. July. 1938. (ERK)

The CAMBRIA leaving Swansea in 1938. (HGO)

The DEVONIA leaving Padstow. Sunday 7th. August 1938. (SR)

Passengers disembarking from the WESTWARD HO at Clovelly in the late 1930's. (HGO)

The GLEN GOWER arriving at Brighton for the round trip to Bristol. Monday 3rd. October 1938. (HGO)

Aboard the GLEN GOWER off the Isle of Wight on the round trip. Monday 3rd. October 1938. Ropes and other moveable items have been removed from the bow and stern and secured amidships. (HGO)

The gale reaches its height on the afternoon of Monday 3rd. October 1938. Everything has now been removed from the foredeck, including the rail seats. (HGO)

The GLEN GOWER stormbound at Southampton. Wednesday 5th. October 1938. (HGO)

CAMPBELL'S SAILINGS

(Weather and Circumstances permitting)

from **Swansea** SOUTH DOCK ENTRANCE, & **Mumbles Pier**

WHITSUN HOLIDAY PROGRAMME
May 26th to June 1st inclusive

---

(6)

CAMPBELL'S SAILINGS

(Weather and Circumstances permitting)

FROM

BRIGHTON (PALACE AND WEST PIERS)

BY THE SALOON STEAMERS

B'TON QUEEN
GLEN GOWER
WAVERLEY

SEASON 1939

AUG. 6th to AUG. 21st inclusive

Booklet timetables for the 1939 season.

The DEVONIA laid up in Bristol. Sunday 12th. February 1939. At the stern are the two lifeboats which were newly fitted for the previous season. (ERK)

The BRIGHTON BELLE leaving Weston. 1939. (ERK)

The RAVENSWOOD and GLEN AVON at Barry. 1939. (ERK)

The GLEN USK in the Cumberland Basin, Bristol. Saturday 20th. May 1939. (ERK)

A "Box Brownie" photograph taken by a youngster in June 1939. The BRIGHTON BELLE in the River Usk, passing John Cashmore's yard where the Union Castle liner, BALMORAL CASTLE, is in the early stages of being broken up. (BMC)

"The Bristol Channel & District Guide" became the "White Funnel Handbook" in 1938 when it included details of the South Coast operations. The 1939 cover is shown above.

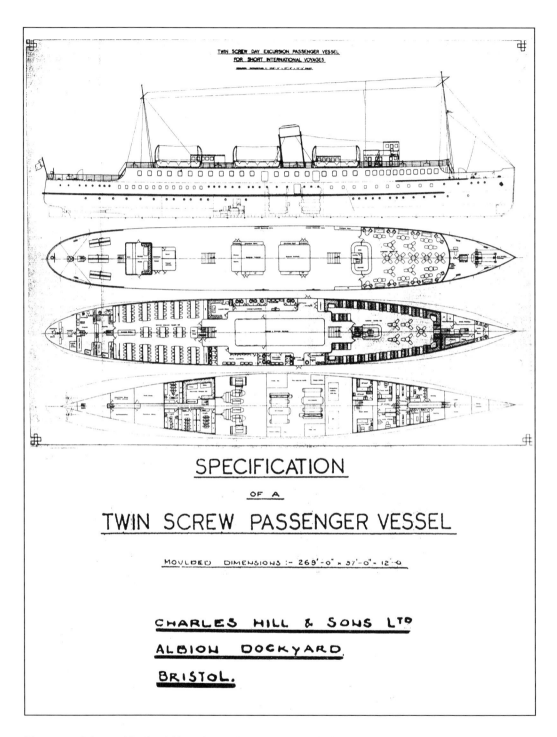

The cover of the specification folder submitted to P. & A. Campbell Ltd. by Charles Hill & Sons. in 1939. Their estimate was rejected.

CAMPBELL'S AMENDED SAILINGS

(Weather and other circumstances permitting) *between*

CARDIFF and WESTON

September 7th to 30th, 1939

OWING TO RESTRICTIONS THIS IS OUR ONLY STEAMER SERVICE :: NOW IN OPERATION ::

		LEAVE CARDIFF	LEAVE WESTON
Th. Sat.	7	10.30 a.m., 2.30 p.m.	11.30 a.m., 3.30 p.m.
Fri.	,, 8	No Sailings.	
Sat.	,, 9	10.50 a.m., 2.45 p.m., 5.0 p.m.	11.50 a.m., 3.45 p.m., 6.15 p.m.
Sun.	,, 10	12.45 p.m., 3.0 p.m., 5.15 p.m.	2.0 p.m., 4.0 p.m., 6.30 p.m.
Mon.	,, 11	2.20 p.m., 5.15 p.m.	3.20 p.m., 6.30 p.m.
Tues.	,, 12	9.0 a.m., 5.15 p.m.	3.15 p.m., 6.30 p.m.
Wed.	,, 13	9.30 a.m., 5.15 p.m.	4.0 p.m., 6.30 p.m.
Thur.	,, 14	9.15 a.m., 5.15 p.m.	10.15 a.m., 6.30 p.m.
Fri.	,, 15	9.15 a.m., 11.15 a.m.	10.15 a.m., 6.0 p.m.
Sat.	,, 16	9.45 a.m., 11.45 a.m.	10.45 a.m., 6.15 p.m.
Sun.	,, 17	10.30 a.m., 12.30 p.m.	11.30 a.m., 6.40 p.m.
Mon.	,, 18	9.30 a.m., 12.0 Noon	10.30 a.m., 1.30 p.m.
Tues.	,, 19	No Sailings this day.	
Wed.	,, 20	9.45 a.m., 11.45 a.m.	10.45 a.m., 3.0 p.m.
Thur.	,, 21	9.45 a.m., 2.30 p.m.	10.45 a.m., 4.0 p.m.
Fri.	,, 22	10.30 a.m., 2.30 p.m.	11.30 a.m., 5.30 p.m.
Sat.	,, 23	10.45 a.m., 2.30 p.m., 5.0 p.m.	11.45 a.m., 3.30 p.m., 6.0 p.m.
Sun.	,, 24	12.40 p.m., 2.40 p.m., 5.0 p.m.	1.40 p.m., 3.40 p.m., 6.0 p.m.
Mon.	,, 25	8.30 a.m., 2.30 p.m.	1.30 p.m., 5.45 p.m.
Tues.	,, 26	9.15 a.m., 3.30 p.m.	2.30 p.m., 5.45 p.m.
Wed.	,, 27	9.45 a.m., 4.15 p.m.	3.0 p.m., 5.45 p.m.
Thur.	,, 28	9.0 a.m., 4.15 p.m.	10.0 a.m., 5.45 p.m.
Fri.	,, 29	No Sailings this day.	
Sat.	,, 30	9.0 a.m., 11.15 a.m.	10.0 a.m., 5.45 p.m.

FARES

Single Journey 3/- Day Return 3/6

Children over 3 and under 14 years half-fare. Dogs, Bicycles, or Prams (at Owners' risk) 2/–, Tandems 3/– Single or Day Return.

Notice as to Conditions.—All Tickets are issued, and passengers carried subject to the Company's conditions as exhibited at the Company's Offices, and on their Steamers.

The Company cannot convey motor cycles or side cars. A reasonable quantity of luggage (which must be labelled) carried free of charge at Passenger's own risk.

For further information apply at the Company's Offices :
1, STUART STREET, CARDIFF .. Tel. 789
PIER GATES, BIRNBECK, WESTON ,, 44
Head Office : CUMBERLAND BASIN, BRISTOL ,, 23112

C. J. Mason & Sons, Printers, Bristol, 1.

The final timetable for 1939, advertising trips which, in the event, never took place.

EPILOGUE

The opening shots of World War Two were fired at dawn on Friday 1st. September when, only a week after the signing of the Anglo/Polish Agreement of assistance, German troops crossed the Polish frontier.

The P. & A. Campbell memorandum book entries for Saturday 2nd. September are headed, "Restricted services operational from this date". The declaration of war was expected at any time. The three south coast steamers were ordered to return to Bristol, all their further sailings were cancelled and they left Newhaven, light, at about 09.30 on the Saturday morning. Just after mid-day they were stopped by an examination vessel, already in position in St. Helens Roads, to the NE of the Isle of Wight, then proceeded outside the island and along the coast, rounding Land's End at about midnight.

In the Bristol Channel the **BRITANNIA** arrived at Bristol at 22.00 after a day trip to Ilfracombe; the **CAMBRIA** and **GLEN USK** berthed at the Pier Head, Cardiff, after a day on the ferry, and the **WESTWARD HO** arrived at Swansea from Ilfracombe. The **BRIGHTON BELLE**, **RAVENSWOOD** and **GLEN AVON,** having been withdrawn from service, had made their way to Bristol earlier in the day to lay up.

On the morning of Sunday 3rd. September the **WESTWARD HO** sailed light from Swansea, stopping, at 07.50, for the examination vessel off Barry, before proceeding to Bristol.

Overnight, the three south coast steamers had made their way homeward in convoy. At precisely 09.00 the **BRIGHTON QUEEN** and **WAVERLEY** were lying at Ilfracombe pier, while the **GLEN GOWER** rounded Bull Point.

At the same time, the British Ambassador in Berlin delivered an ultimatum to the German government, stating that unless German troops were withdrawn from Poland, a state of war would exist between Great Britain and Germany.

The ultimatum expired at 11.00. Fifteen minutes later, the Prime Minister, in a radio broadcast, informed the nation that no reply had been received and that, as a consequence, the country was at war.

For the White Funnel Fleet, it marked the end of another era and for the second time in its history, the company prepared for conflict.

INDEX *Figures in italics refer to illustrations*

205

SUBSCRIBERS

Presentation copies

1. Mr. George Owen.   2. Mr. Nigel Coombes.   3. Bristol Records Office.

4 Raymond Wood
5 W. S. Vanstone
6 Paul Steeds
7 Paul Steeds
8 Mr. Ken Saunders
9 Mr. G. J. Shaw
10 Michael Sullivan
11 John K. W. Slater
12 Mike Riley
13 Michael Perrins
14 G. W. Pritchard
15 Martin Nelson
16 Michael Mason
17 Geoffrey C. Lidstone
18 John G. Lidstone
19 Tom S. B. Lee
20 G. E. Jefferies
21 Mr. G. A. Jacobs
22 Christopher Henton
23 T. S. Howard
24 J. P. Henworth
25 G. A. Gough
26 P. J. Fricker
27 R. A. Fenner
28 Eric Freeman
29 J. Donaldson
30 Tom Baker
31 Peter Clark
32 Derek Crawford
33 R. W. Beesley
34 Charles Brown
35 Lt. Cdr. R. K. P. Abbot, RNR
36 D. J. Browning
37 Dr. D. J. Anderson
38 H. W. West
39 Mr. R. H. Turner
40 David Tribe
41 Mark Stockdale
42 Peter Stocker
43 John Salvage
44 L. Gordon Reed
45 M. Oatway
46 Andrew P. Munn
47 Derek Warman
48 David Beeney
49 Peter Manton King
50 D. R. Morris
51 Alastair Wm. McRobb
52 Peter Lucas
53 John Kelly, BEM and
     Jenny Kelly
54 P. D. A. Joziasse
55 Rev. Jack House
56 G. F. A. Gilbert
57 Mr. K. F. Floyd
58 Kenneth Fraser
59 James A Fisher
60 Roger F. V. Edlin
61 Terry Cresswell
62 Richard Clammer

63 Jeff Bishop
64 A. J. Brown
65 David J. Barton
66 Hammy Sparks
67 Norman Partyn
68 Cecil H. Pearce
69 Harold Mills
70 Mrs. N. Lacey
71 David A. Jones
72 Don K. Jones
73 Keith Hooper
74 W. Haydn Burgess
75 Ivor Davies (Oxford)
76 Alister Currie
77 Crawford Alexander
78 E. P. Allen
79 M. H. and J. R. Adams
80 K. M. Adams
81 Alan Wakeman
82 George C. Train
83 J. L. Stanfield
84 Ian Ramsay
85 Barry Le Jeune
86 Elizabeth Gillard
87 Ian Boyle
88 G. G. Boswell
89 Clive Seaton
90 Mrs. I. Smele
91 Robert Pinfield
92 Neil O'Brien,
     Purser MV Balmoral
93 H. R. A. Mills
94 Dr. W. Marshall Walker
95 Alastair Reid McMillan
96 R. G. Lewis
97 Alec Lewis
98 N. Jones
99 Kenneth Howell
100 Richard Eaves
101 Brian Elliott
102 Alan Downs
103 Kenneth John Campbell
104 Sqn. Ldr. Alan Birt
105 M. C. Banks
106 The Revd. Norman Bird
107 Anthony J. Morgan
108 P. Brocklesby
109 Stephen J. Wilson
110 Mr. R. E. Tudball
111 Victor Gray
112 Derek W. Spiers
113 Dr. Doug Naysmith, MP
114 Peter K. Massey
115 M. J. Williams
116 J. L. May
117 Dr. D. J. Herriot
118 Tony Glasson
119 J. Graeme Bruce
120 P. E. Cox
121 J. White

122 Keith Draper
123 Bob Coles
124 Mr. Alan T. Bridges
125 Colin Simpson
126 Clive Staddon
127 J. R. Logan
128 Tom Allison
129 A. D. Knox
130 Bernard A. Barry
131 Alan Wilson
132 John Spears
133 D. A. Dickman
134 Mike Tedstone
135 Bryn May
136 John and Elizabeth Holmes
137 Roy N. Pedersen
138 F. W. Hann
139 Rev. A. W. Huckett
140 Andrew M. Gully
141 M. T. Parry
142 David Docherty
143 John and Myra Allen
144 Alan Brown
145 Noel Johnson
146 Sidney W. Robinson
147 J. N. Woodman
148 Keith Thomas
149 Brian Patton
150 E. J. Wilson
151 Anthony Michael Horn
152 Ashley Gill
153 Brian M. Whitmore
154 E. G. Davis
155 Hilda Guns, nee Parker
156 Brian Fisher
157 Miss M. H. Pook
158 Eric H. Chamberlain
159 R. S. Turner
160 Eric J. Tilly
161 Douglas McGowan
162 R. G. Danielson
163 R. A. Durston
164 K. W. Jenkins
165 F. D. Ramsden
166 M. A. James
167 Capt. E. Davies
168 P. G. and E. M. Boldero
169 Mr. & Mrs. W. T. Collard
170 Ken and Rita Williams
171 Roger Nowell
172 Richard Johnson
173 Mr. K. T. Allwright
174 Mr. David Burt
175 Mr. Alfred Harvey
176 Peter Southcombe
177 Richard Havard
178 T. G. Richards
179 J. Forster-Brown
180 Mr. F. M. Smith

P. & A. CAMPBELL LTD.

1929

Long Afternoon Channel Cruise
around the
SCARWEATHER LIGHTSHIP

By the magnificent Saloon Steamer

"LADY MOYRA"

(Weather and Circumstances permitting),

THURSDAY, JULY 18th

LEAVING PORTHCAWL 3.35 p.m. Arriving back
about 5.10 p.m. **Special Fare 1s. 6d.**
(Children under 14 Half-price).

**Passengers having small parcels of
Newspapers and Books for the Crew of
the Lightship will be able to see them
put on board. (Weather permitting).**

Refreshments of all kinds supplied at Moderate Charges.

For Further Particulars apply

"NEWS OFFICE," PORTHCAWL.

Dates, Ltd., Printers, Cardiff.